Our Modern Stone Age

Our Modern Stone Age

Robert L. Bates

Julia A. Jackson

William Kaufmann, Inc.

Los Altos, California

Persons and organizations that have provided photographs for this book:

American Aggregates Corporation
Buckeye Steel Castings Company
Cargill, Inc.
Domtar Industries Inc.
English China Clays Group
The Feldspar Corporation
Florida Phosphate Council
Freeport Sulphur Company
General Electric Company
General Refractories Company
Georgia Marble Company
W. R. Grace & Company
Houdaille Construction Materials, Inc.
Illinois State Geological Survey
Indiana Geological Survey
Johns-Manville Canada Inc.
Johns-Manville Sales Corporation
S. J. Lefond
L. E. Mannion
J. D. Martinez
Martin Marietta Cement
Maury Drenkel, Inc.
Monsanto Company
Morton Salt Division of MortonNorwich

National Gallery of Art
National Lime Association
National Limestone Institute
Ohio Geological Survey
Perlite Institute
Peter Silveri Associates, Inc.
Portland Cement Association
PPG Industries Inc.
Royal Botanical Gardens (Hamilton, Ontario)
Saskatchewan Mineral Resources
Shell Photographic Service
Stauffer Chemical Company of Wyoming
Truman Stauffer, Sr.
Steuben Glass
United States Borax & Chemical Corporation
United States Bureau of Mines
United States Department of Housing
  and Urban Development
United States Geological Survey
United States Gypsum Company
J. D. Vineyard
Yara Engineering Corporation

The line drawings are by Ron Lieser

*Designed by David Mike Hamilton. Page layout by Spectra
Media. Composed in phototype Oracle and Goudy Handtooled
by Publishing Services Center. Printed on seventy-pound
Michigan Matte by Braun-Brumfield, Inc. in an edition of
3,500 copies.*

Library of Congress Cataloging in Publication Data

*Bates, Robert Latimer, 1912–
  Our modern stone age.*

  *Bibliography: p.
  Includes index.
  1. Nonmetallic minerals. I. Jackson, Julia Andreasen,
1939– . II. Title.
TN799.5.B37   553.6   81-17219
ISBN 0-86576-027-6   AACR2*

10 9 8 7 6 5 4 3 2 1

Contents

Preface

To enjoy this book, you need only a little time and a little curiosity about rocks and minerals and how we use them.

The odds are at least 100 to 1 that you never heard of *trona*. They are also high that your kitchen cupboards are stocked with products made from it. Trona is a mineral—natural sodium carbonate. It is an essential ingredient of glass, soap, detergents, water softeners, washing soda, baking soda, and paper products. Mined only since 1946, in Wyoming, trona has taken over the domestic market for sodium carbonate from a long-established industry that made it synthetically. It is even making inroads into this industry in Europe. Trona is a strong exception to the rule that says manufactured products tend to replace natural ones in the market place.

Trona is one of about 35 nonmetallic rocks and minerals of importance in our economy. We refer to the group simply as *nonmetallics*, or, since they are used mostly in industry, as *industrial rocks and minerals*. Besides helping to stock our kitchen cupboards, these earth materials fertilize the nation's croplands, insulate homes, sharpen machine tools, filter liquids, fill plastics and paper, melt ice on roads, and go into the making of chemicals, film, paint, dyes, fireworks, and a long list of other items, including the tube in your TV set.

Each year in the United States we use 11 tons of nonmetallic earth materials for every man, woman, and child. In contrast, we use only two-thirds of a ton of metals. Yet the metals outshine the nonmetallics in the news, and in our consciousness, because metals are recognizable in the final product. Most nonmetallics are used up at some stage of manufacture, like limestone in the smelting of iron ores, or clay in the drilling of oil wells. Or they may be converted into new and different compounds, as happens with bright yellow sulfur. More than four-fifths of this mineral survives only as far as the plant where it is made into sulfuric acid. This acid, and the remaining sulfur, are used in making scores of consumer products, but we see no trace of sulfur in the tires, paper, detergents, and other items that it helps to produce. Most of the nonmetallics lose their identity somewhere between mine or quarry and the products that we see and use.

In this book we describe about two dozen rocks and minerals: how they occur, how they are extracted from the ground and moved about the earth's surface, and what happens to them in the labyrinth of industry. We also look at problems of energy consumption, and especially at the environmental restraints under which mineral producers must now do business. You may find that knowing something about these subjects will help you to make informed decisions on mineral or energy policies. Our main purpose, however, is simply to share with you our fascination with these earth-derived materials and their place in our complex society.

Robert L. Bates
Julia A. Jackson
August 1981

1.

Our Modern Stone Age

Each year every American consumes, on the average, 93 pounds of sugar. We also use up several hundred gallons of gasoline, and 1½ pairs of shoes. And we really do consume these things: we eat the sugar, burn the gasoline, and wear out the shoes. The thought gives us comfort: the welfare of our country rests on the shoulders of the great American consumer. We're the people behind the Gross National Product.

The 11-Ton-Per-Year Consumer

Each of us also "consumes" immense amounts of earth materials—though in a somewhat different way from candy bars or shoes. Can you imagine receiving your annual quota of rocks, minerals,

More than 22,000 pounds of nonfuel earth materials are required annually for every U.S. citizen. About 94 percent are nonmetallics. (U.S. Bureau of Mines.)

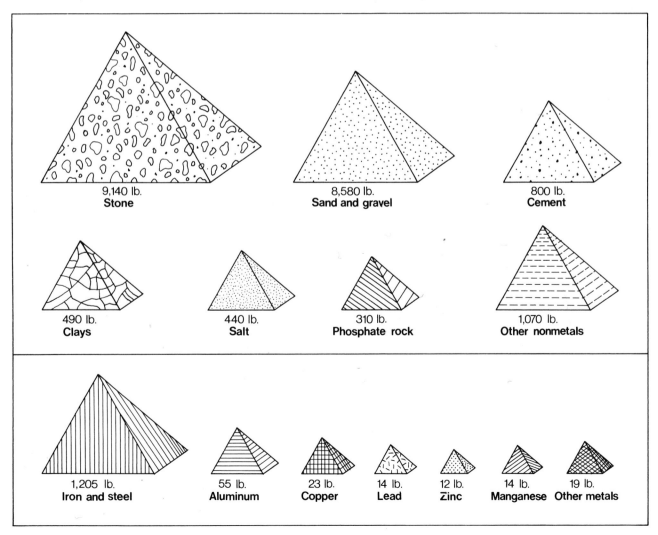

9,140 lb.
Stone

8,580 lb.
Sand and gravel

800 lb.
Cement

490 lb.
Clays

440 lb.
Salt

310 lb.
Phosphate rock

1,070 lb.
Other nonmetals

1,205 lb.
Iron and steel

55 lb.
Aluminum

23 lb.
Copper

14 lb.
Lead

12 lb.
Zinc

14 lb.
Manganese

19 lb.
Other metals

and metals in a single delivery? A large truck pulls up in front of your property, and the driver unloads:

9,140 pounds of stone
8,580 pounds of sand and gravel
800 pounds of cement
490 pounds of clay
440 pounds of salt
310 pounds of phosphate rock
1,070 pounds of other nonmetals
1,342 pounds of metals

A patented "stone-breaker" from 1858. Chunks of rock were fed by hand into a crusher powered by a steam engine. Coarse fragments fell into the cart, finer ones into two bins below the tubular screen. This was a tremendous advance over breaking stone by hand. (Courtesy of National Limestone Institute.)

An identical shipment—over 22,000 pounds, or 11 tons—would be made once a year for every man, woman, and child in the country.

The figures are obtained by dividing the country's total consumption of earth materials by the number of people. Such a procedure reduces the enormous total—some 2 billion tons—to figures that we can at least roughly comprehend. But how does each of us "consume" 11 tons of rocks, minerals, and metals in a year? Where do they all go?

The top three entries on the list make up 84 percent of the total. Combined in the form of concrete—a manmade stone—they are essential for all construction. Cement, the ingredient that makes concrete "set" to rocklike hardness, is manufactured from limestone and shale. Some 90 million tons is produced each year. Sand (fine aggregate) and gravel or crushed stone (coarse aggregate) give concrete its volume and strength. A single mile of four-lane highway, with bridges and interchanges, requires 85,000 tons of aggregate. Even an average house requires 50 tons. So by far the biggest users of earth materials are the industries that build our homes and highways (not to mention shopping malls, office buildings, and airports). It is no exaggeration to say that we live in an age of stone.

Clay, the next item on the list, is used to make brick and tile; in addition, much high-quality white clay goes into fine china, and into shiny paper for picture books and magazines. As for that 440 pounds of salt, perhaps 1 percent will end up on the table of the ultimate consumer, but most of it will be used for control of ice on winter roads, and in the manufacture of some 75 sodium and chlorine chemicals. The phosphate is used as fertilizer, mostly by large "agribusiness" firms. Hidden in the 1,070 pounds of other nonmetals are some 30 rocks and minerals with special or unique properties that make them of value, for example the industrial diamond. Modern high-speed precision methods of manufacture may be said to rest ultimately on the cutting edge of this ultra-hard mineral.

The last entry on the list is rather a surprise: iron, copper, aluminum, and the other metals make up only 6 percent of the total. Important as the metals are in construction and industry, they are far outweighed by the nonmetallic materials.

Limestone: Our Most Versatile Raw Material

Rocks, along with the minerals and fossils they contain, are the chief records of earth history. As such, they form the subject matter of half a dozen related sciences. But rocks are not considered from that viewpoint here: our concern is solely with practical use. If a rock is useful, we're interested; otherwise, no. In commercial parlance, rock becomes *stone*.

The most versatile and widely used rock in the earth's crust is limestone. A sedimentary rock, limestone began its existence as a layer of shells and limy mud on the floor of an ancient sea. In the course of geologic time, the layer became buried by younger strata and hardened into rock. Eventually the sea floor was uplifted and the sea withdrew. Erosion exposed the limestone and its accompanying rocks on the landscape as we see them today.

Pure limestone is made of only one mineral, calcite, a compound known chemically as calcium carbonate, $CaCO_3$. But the pure rock is rare. Most limestones contain other minerals, such as particles of clay and grains of quartz. Limestone may be dense and fine-grained, granular like sugar, or an aggregate of calcite crystals up to a quarter of an inch in diameter. Although some limestones contain enough organic matter to make them dark gray or even black, the most common colors are light gray to tan. Many are thin-bedded and slabby, some occur in beds a foot or two thick, and a few are in massive uniform beds from which big blocks can be quarried. Well-preserved fossils are present in some limestones, but in others the sea shells were ground up by the waves of the parent sea before the sediment became rock.

Crushed and ground stone. At a typical limestone quarry, the rock is blasted down and fed to crushers; the crushed stone is then separated into various sizes by screening. Limestone's structure of interlocking calcite grains makes the fragments strong and gives them a high resistance to freezing and thawing. The stone doesn't produce enough quartz dust to abrade quarry machinery or scar the workmen's lungs. Limestone is widely distributed, and deposits are likely to be available where needed. For all these reasons, more than twice as much limestone is used as all other rock types combined.

Crushed and screened limestone, for concrete aggregate. (Courtesy of National Limestone Institute.)

The major market is our seemingly endless demand for concrete aggregate. This will continue as long as we build more miles of freeway and more acres of housing developments and office complexes.

At some plants, the stone is not merely crushed but pulverized. The resulting dust ("aglime") is spread on crop land as a soil conditioner. Light-colored limestone of high purity is ground extremely fine to a white powder, which is used in a variety of products, especially paint and plastics.

Dimension stone. A few limestone deposits consist of thick massive beds, without fractures or other partings. Such deposits yield blocks that can be sawed, smoothed, turned, or carved for use in buildings or in monuments and memorials. A light-colored stone in uniform beds as much as 30 feet thick, near Bloomington in southern Indiana, has been quarried for dimension stone since 1827. (This area was the site of the 1979 film *Breaking Away*.) Blocks are carefully cut by channeling machines and loosened from the quarry floor. Then they are taken to the mill, where they are fashioned to order according to specifications of

Old times: putting pulverized limestone ("aglime") on the land. (Courtesy of National Limestone Institute.)

Quarrying Indiana limestone. The straight cuts are made by steam channeling machines (beyond the derrick). Long blocks, freed at the bottom, are "turned down" and split into smaller blocks for removal to the finishing plant. (Indiana Geological Survey.)

the architect or designer. This light gray or tan "Indiana limestone" is a familiar sight on large buildings, from university libraries to office towers.

Quite a different stone is quarried near Knoxville, Tennessee. This is a pale pink to chocolate-brown limestone. It has a coarsely crystalline texture, and therefore, unlike the Indiana stone, will take a polish. Prominent on the surfaces of this "Tennessee marble" are dark-gray lines that look like earthquake records on a seismogram, or heartbeats on a cardiogram. Called *stylolites*, they record an interval of pressure and solution when the rock was young. The stone is used mostly for interiors, especially in floors, panels, and window sills. A striking application of Tennessee marble is on the East Building of the U.S. National Gallery of Art in Washington, D.C., completed in 1977. Both inside and outside walls of this structure are faced with the Tennessee stone, rough-finished rather than polished.

Much dimension limestone is beautiful, and it's all interesting because we see the rock itself instead of some product made from it. But the amount of such stone produced is only a tiny fraction of the country's total limestone tonnage. (Consider its competition—concrete, brick, glass.) Several fundamental uses of limestone depend on the chemistry of $CaCO_3$ rather than the physical properties of the rock.

Raw material of cement.

"Take two cups of crushed limestone; add one-half cup of clay or pulverized shale (plus

East building, National Gallery of Art, Washington, D.C. The building is faced with light pinkish gray limestone from Tennessee. (Courtesy of the National Gallery of Art.)

perhaps some sandstone or iron ore, depending); mix thoroughly and grind up fine. Bake in white-hot oven at about 1427°C (2600°F). Cool. Add a tablespoonful of gypsum, and, again, grind very fine."

This recipe, which was presented a few years ago by a professor of engineering with tongue in cheek, gives in capsule form the essentials of cement manufacture. Multiply the quantities by a couple of million and you have some idea of what is handled at a cement plant *every day*. More than 150 plants, in 50 states, produce about 90 million tons of cement annually. Worldwide, there are 1,700 plants in 120 countries.

Four parts of high-purity limestone are carefully proportioned with one part of clay or shale, plus a little iron oxide or silica if needed. (At a few places, impure limestone is found that contains just about the right proportions of clay. This "cement limestone" is then the chief raw material.) However derived, the mixture is ground to flour. It is then fed into the upper end of a slightly inclined and slowly rotating steel tube that is lined with heat-resistant brick. Some of these rotary kilns—as much as 25 feet in diameter and 760 feet long—are the largest single units of moving machinery in industrial use. The charge moves gradually down the kiln under gravity toward the lower end. Here an intense heat is produced by combustion of gas or powdered coal. Tongues of flame may reach 30 or 40 feet into the kiln. In the heat blast, at a maximum temperature of about 1600°C (2912°F)—somewhat hotter than specified in the professor's recipe—the kiln charge is partly melted. It emerges as a glassy clinker. After cooling, the clinker is mixed with 2 to 4 percent of gypsum and is ground extremely fine. The resulting gray powder is finished cement.

No chemists are crawling around in the kiln in all that heat, but what apparently happens is this. The calcium carbonate of the limestone breaks down into carbon dioxide, which escapes as a gas, and calcium oxide, or lime, which remains. This com-

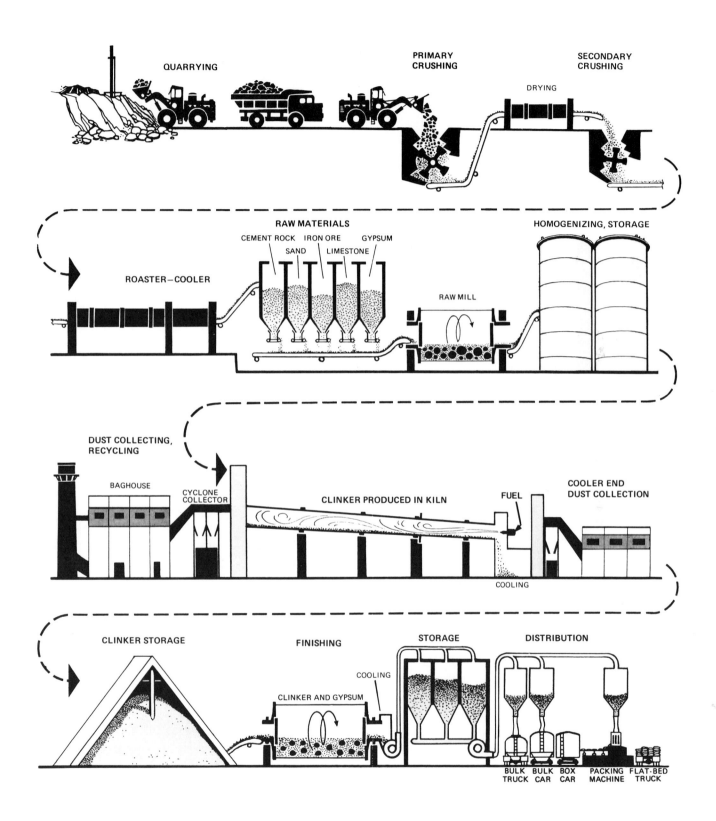

An energy-intensive process: the making of cement. Heart of the operation is the kiln, where intense heat converts the raw material in- *to clinker. Much additional energy is required for crushing, drying, and fine-grinding. (Courtesy of Martin Marietta Cement.)*

bines with alumina and silica from the clay or shale to form new compounds, calcium aluminates and silicates, in the clinker and so in the cement. These compounds, when powdered and mixed with water, will "set" to rocklike firmness. The gypsum that is added helps regulate the setting time. As we have noted, cement is the active ingredient of concrete, the indispensable construction material. That simple recipe, then—four-fifths of which is limestone—is the basis of an immense segment of industry.

Source of lime. *Lime* is an ancient word, derived from the Latin word *limus* for mud or mire, probably in reference to lime mortar or plaster. Only stone and clay are more venerable in use than lime mortar. It holds together the Great Wall of China; in Roman times it was used in roads, aqueducts, and coliseums. Lime plaster, dating to 4000 B.C., has been found in the pyramids of Egypt. As recently as the early 1900s, more than 80 percent of the lime produced in this country was used in

plaster, but this application has been largely taken over by gypsum. Lime is now used in a wide range of chemical and industrial processes. Indeed, lime is second only to sulfuric acid as an "intermediate chemical" of modern industry, being used somewhere along the line between raw material and finished product but seldom showing up in the latter.

What is this ancient and adaptable material, which gave its name to the stone from which it is produced?

If we take 100 pounds of crushed pure limestone ($CaCO_3$) and heat it in a kiln by direct exposure to flame at about 1093°C (2000°F), 44 pounds will disappear as carbon dioxide gas, CO_2, and 56 pounds will remain as white porous lumps of calcium oxide, CaO. This is known as lime, or, more precisely, as *quicklime*. If left alone, especially in the presence of moisture, CaO tends to absorb CO_2 from the air and revert to its original carbonate form. Being thus perishable, quicklime

A cement manufacturing plant. Raw materials, stored in two silos at top of view, are blended in tall building and introduced into kiln. Clinker, produced in kiln, is ground to cement in building at left. Con- *veyor leads to loading facility, partly shown at front edge of view. Shed at upper left is for clinker storage. (Courtesy of Portland Cement Association.)*

Concrete in one of its many uses. The bridge crosses Pine Valley Creek, 40 miles east of San Diego, California. (Courtesy of Portland Cement Association.)

must be stored in dry, water-tight containers. A more stable form is *hydrated lime*. To produce this, we add 18 pounds of water to the 56 pounds of quicklime that we first obtained, ending up with 74 pounds of hydrated lime, $Ca(OH)_2$, plus some heat.

Lime in both its forms is widely used. We have space to list only the more important applications of this versatile spin-off of limestone. Lime is used in—

Steel manufacture. In the molten steel, quicklime acts as a scavenger, or flux, by combining with silica, alumina, phosphorus, and sulfur to form a silicate slag, which is drawn off. An average of 150 pounds of lime is used for every ton of steel produced.

Water treatment. In combination with another chemical, sodium carbonate, lime softens drinking water for municipal systems. It also helps control bacteria, and clarifies water by making suspended solids settle out.

Treatment of sewage and industrial wastes. Here lime helps remove compounds that contain phosphorus and nitrogen. These compounds are undesirable in sewage-plant effluents, because they promote the growth of algae in lakes and ponds. Lime is also used in treating the wastes from chemical and pharmaceutical plants and paper mills.

"Scrubbing" smokestack gases. Several techniques have been developed for removing sulfur dioxide (SO_2) from the gases that go up the smokestack at big coal-burning power plants. Most of these techniques involve lime. In one method, the smoke and gas rises through a spray, or "slurry," of lime plus water. The pollutant gases become entrained in the droplets of slurry, fall to the bottom of the column, and are removed as an impure calcium-sulfate sludge. Lime is needed because it readily combines with the SO_2.

Neutralizing acid mine drainage. Waters draining from active and abandoned coal mines are likely to contain compounds of iron and sulfur—produced by weathering of pyrite in the coal and adjacent strata. These acid compounds

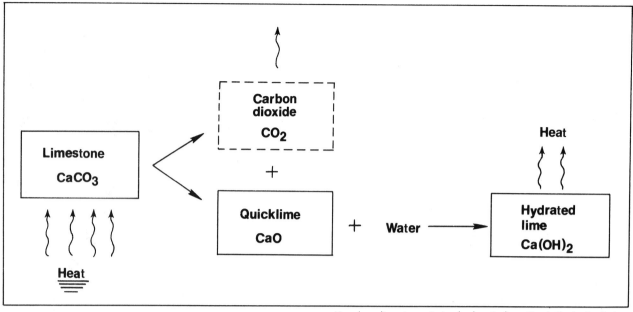

Lime from limestone. A simple chemical reaction is the basis of a large and important industry.

may be neutralized by treatment with hydrated lime.

The manufacture of chemicals. Lime is used in the production of bleaches, calcium-phosphate fertilizers, chrome chemicals, pesticides, paint pigments, and a variety of organic chemicals.

Papermaking. In the manufacture of kraft paper (brown wrapping paper, shopping bags, and the like), quicklime regenerates the key chemical, caustic soda, for re-use in a continuous process.

Glass. Lime is one of the three main constituents of bottle glass and ordinary window glass, the others being sand (silica) and soda ash (sodium carbonate).

Food processing. In a sugar refinery, the crude juice is treated with lime. This combines with phosphates and organic compounds to produce solids that can be removed by filtering. About 500

USES OF LIMESTONE

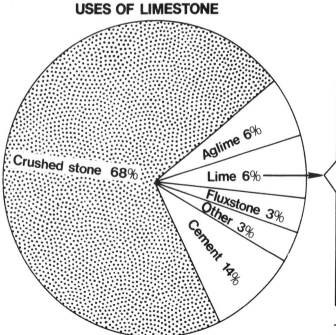

Crushed stone 68%
Aglime 6%
Lime 6%
Fluxstone 3%
Other 3%
Cement 14%

USES OF LIME

In glass
As flux in steelmaking
In alkalies, soda ash, and other chemicals
In water treatment, neutralizing coal-mine waste, scrubbing smokestack gases
In treating pulp for paper manufacture
In sand-lime brick and other refractories
In sugar refining
As a filler in rubber and plastics
As an extender in paint
In mortar, stucco
In soil stabilization
In soil neutralization

Without limestone and lime, industry would come to a halt.

pounds of quicklime is used for every ton of beet sugar. In warehouses where fresh fruit is stored, lime is used to absorb excess carbon dioxide that may build up and promote rotting. Lime is an intermediate chemical in the production of table-grade salt from brines.

Soil stabilization. In the early 1950s it was found that claylike, plastic soil can be made hard and stable by the addition of hydrated lime. This has now become a big market, for stabilizing the clay subgrade or base on which structures are to be built. Lime has been used in at least 2,000 miles of interstate highway. At the Dallas-Fort Worth airport, constructed between 1971 and 1974, about 300,000 tons of hydrated lime was used in pavements and building areas.

Mortar. Most of the mortars in use today are mixtures of cement, lime, and sand; a common proportion is 1:2:9. Lime makes the mortar easy to work, and the cement provides a rapid setting time.

Agriculture. Applied to cropland, lime acts as a plant nutrient and helps neutralize acidity. Although more expensive than ground limestone, it reacts with the soil more rapidly and allows rapid turnover of crops.

Life without limestone? Practical usefulness, we said earlier, is what a rock or mineral must possess to merit our attention in this book. Limestone—crushed, ground, powdered, cut, sawed, or polished; calcined alone to make lime or calcined with shale to make cement—is the pre-eminent example of usefulness. This rock and its derivatives permeate the whole fabric of our society.

Energy Requirements

Stretching across the southern end of San Francisco Bay is a series of low dikes enclosing shallow rectangular ponds. Here sea water evaporates and salt is recovered, in a manner that has been in use for centuries and is still practiced at many localities in the world. The salt thus produced—"solar salt"—is one of the few mineral materials that we acquire with no application of nonrenewable energy. Except for maintaining the ponds and harvesting the salt, the sun does it all.

Nearly all our industrial rocks and minerals require an input of energy before they can be used—some less, some more. Among those with

Soil stabilization. Hydrated lime will be mixed with the soil and compacted into a hard all-weather surface. This is part of an airport project. (Courtesy of National Lime Association.)

the lowest requirements are crushed stone, sand, and gravel. This is fortunate, considering the enormous tonnages of these materials that are produced. It costs something to crush stone and to screen sand and gravel, but neither product requires fine grinding or the application of heat—the two big users of energy. Somewhat more energy must be expended on gypsum, a sedimentary rock that goes into plasterboard. The raw gypsum must first be ground up, and then heated to drive off a part of its combined water, leaving plaster of paris. Mixed with water, this plaster is then sandwiched between sheets of heavy paper. In a highly mechanized process, a continuous sheet of this wallboard sandwich passes through an oven to dry and harden the plaster. So both grinding and heat are involved. To produce a ton of gypsum wallboard requires the equivalent of about 750 kilowatt-hours (kwh) of energy. (If you use a 1,000-watt electric heater for one hour, you consume 1 kwh of energy.) This means that to produce every pound of wallboard in your house required the energy of 1,000 watts for 22½ minutes.

Perhaps, as we talk of energy, you recall that cement kiln with its temperature of 1600°C (2912°F).

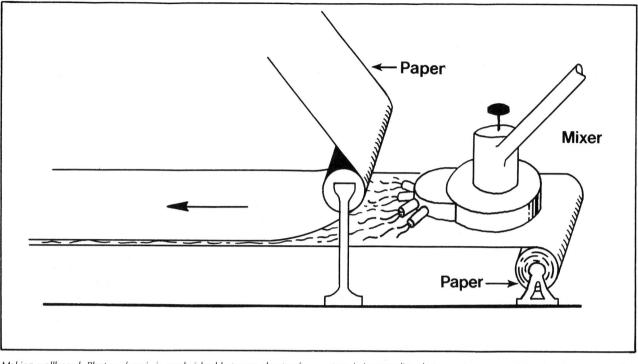

Making wallboard. Plaster of paris is sandwiched between sheets of heavy paper on an automated production line. This stage of manufac- ture is intermediate between two energy-intensive stages: preparing the plaster from raw gypsum and drying the wallboard in a kiln.

Not only is a tremendous amount of energy expended here, but the material fed to the kiln must be ground very fine, and so must the clinker that emerges. Thus, the cement industry is extremely energy-intensive. About 1,750 kwh are used for each ton produced. In fact, the part of the selling price that must be ascribed to the cost of energy is higher for cement than for any other nonmetallic manufactured product. The production of lime is similarly energy-intensive.

As might be expected, in recent years producers of these and other nonmetallic products have become much interested in conserving energy. The cement industry has closed old, inefficient plants, and in new plants has introduced better grinding mills, pre-heaters that utilize heat formerly wasted, and various insulating materials. At one plant, a part of the silica-alumina-iron raw material is provided by fly-ash—the fine particles recovered from power-plant smoke. Since this requires no grinding, its use has saved more than 10 kwh of energy per ton of cement produced.

Demand for some nonmetallic materials is increasing because they're needed for energy conservation. Among these are sand, lime, and soda ash, for making glass-fiber insulation; borates to

fireproof the insulation made from shredded paper or other cellulose; and several minerals that are good insulators in themselves. The drive to obtain energy from new sources may increase the demand for some materials derived from industrial minerals, for example, lithium for electric batteries. And at least a dozen industrial minerals are used in the oil industry—that is, in *producing* energy. These range from barite and bentonite, used in drilling, to absorbent clays needed in the refinery.

Incidentally, the energy used in processing the nonmetallics is far less than that required for refining metals. To produce a ton of copper, for example, takes about 10,000 kwh equivalent; to produce a ton of aluminum takes 16,000 kwh, or about 9 times as much as cement. The reason is that it's extremely difficult to separate a single element like copper or aluminum from the complex rock in which it occurs. Furthermore, many of the ores now being worked are very low-grade; the content of metallic copper in most ores mined today is less than one-half of one percent. No wonder it takes so much energy to obtain the shiny pure metal! Of the country's total energy consumption, the metals use 4.7 percent, and the industrial minerals only 1.9 percent.

Environmental Effects

Concern for the environment has an impact on all segments of the minerals industry, from the large international project to the local quarry. We discuss this subject in a later chapter. At this time we just point out that environmentally directed actions decrease the demand for some industrial minerals and increase the demand for others. For example, the ban on fluorocarbons has had an adverse effect on the mining of the mineral fluorspar. If a ban on phosphates in detergents goes into effect, the phosphate-mining industry will be affected. On the other hand, clean-air requirements have opened up a large market for lime and limestone, which are used to remove sulfur dioxide from stack gases at coal-fired power plants.

Still in the Stone Age

Space Age man would seem to have little in common with Stone Age man, whose very name suggests shelter, tools, and weapons made of stone. Yet the crust of the earth yields the materials of our existence today as it did for our remote ancestors. We use sophisticated methods of finding, mining, and processing earth materials; we use far more of them, and we put them to uses undreamed of by early man. As a result, we are even more dependent on the earth's rocky crust than he was. And if the rock or mineral that we need is not at hand, we have a supply sent to us from across town or across the ocean. In the next chapter we look at some of the types of travel that are routine for materials of the modern stone age.

Laying a "base course" of crushed stone for a highway. (Courtesy of National Limestone Institute.)

2.

Rocks en Route

Nothing occurs where it's needed.

Anyone surveying the field of industrial rocks and minerals is bound to reach this conclusion. Whether it's a few miles between quarry and construction project, or several thousand miles between plant and customer, distance seems always to be involved. This fact brings into the picture a fascinating variety of methods for handling and transporting these earth materials.

How much can we spend on getting rocks and minerals from where they're found to where they're needed? Clearly this depends on the value of the material. Gravel and stone are so cheap that they can't be moved very far; as the economist says, "they won't stand high transportation charges." But minerals or rocks with special or unique properties, such as high-grade paper clay or phosphate-rock fertilizer, command high prices and can profitably be moved across continents and oceans. Efforts are always under way to improve procedures in handling and transportation, with a view toward lowering costs per delivered ton. Reduced costs mean that lower grades of material, or more remote deposits, can be exploited. Thus, a better way of packing or moving a rock or mineral may have a pronounced effect on international trade.

In this chapter we explore some of the ingenious ways that have been devised for getting minerals and rocks from here to there.

Limestone by Pipeline

The owners of a cement plant at San Andreas, California, faced a dilemma. In a few years their nearby limestone quarry would be exhausted, and the only feasible replacement was a deposit 17.6 airline miles away. They could dismantle the plant and move it to the new deposit, but this would be time-consuming and extremely expensive. They could bring limestone from the new deposit to the plant by truck, but this would mean hauling it over 24 miles of public roads and through small towns. Instead, they chose to build a pipeline. Constructed in less than a year, the pipeline is entirely under ground, so as not to mar the beauty of the Sierra Nevada foothills. Limestone from the new quarry is crushed, ground, and mixed with water, before it enters the pipe. The slurry reaches the plant just over 4 hours later, having travelled at about the pace of a brisk walk. It is stored in basins at the San Andreas plant and is used as needed.

Slurry pipelines operate at low cost, and they have the least impact on the environment of any mode of transport. On the other hand, a pipeline is a fixed connection between two points and thus is highly inflexible. To lay a line between a mineral producer and a mineral consumer would set up a relationship that would be hard to change if one of the parties wished to change it. So most pipelines, like the California line described above, are "in-house" facilities that take a single material from its source to another place for processing. Another reason why pipelines are rare in general transportation is that they are incompatible with most other transport methods. The solids to be moved must be combined with water at one end and dewatered at the other, so that handling costs are likely to be high.

Miles of Belts

Unlike slurry pipelines, belt conveyors are commonplace. A conveyor simply consists of an

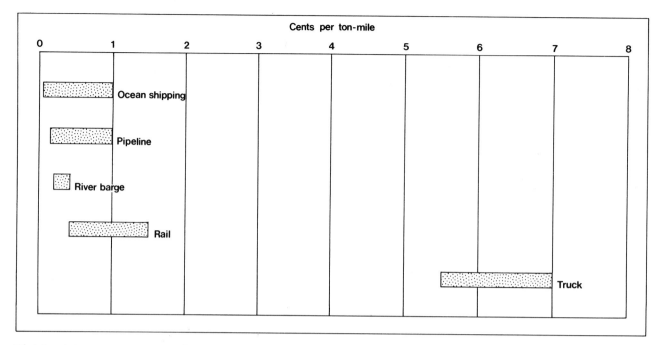

What it costs to move one ton one mile.

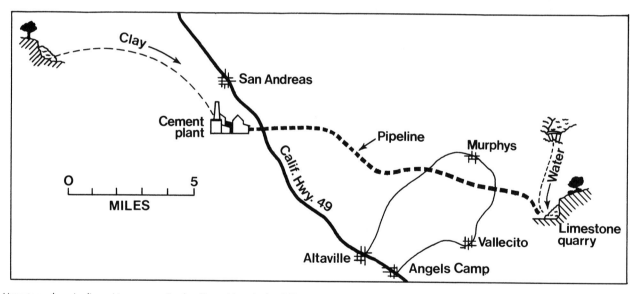

Limestone by pipeline. At a quarry in the Sierra Nevada foothills, California, ground limestone is mixed with water and sent to the cement plant by pipeline. This is cheaper, and has less effect on the environment, than moving crushed stone by truck. (Courtesy of Pit and Quarry.)

endless rubber belt, generally 3 or 4 feet wide and several hundred feet long, half of which at any moment is moving forward on rollers carrying a load (the "top strand"), while the other half returns empty beneath (the "bottom strand"). Power is supplied by electric motors. Many belt systems are permanent installations, forming costly and elegant systems of transport; others, mounted on wheeled frames, can be moved from one part of a pit or quarry to another or taken to a different site.

At Warrenville, Illinois, a sand and gravel company operates a producing pit on the opposite side of the East-West Tollway from the processing plant. (The original deposit next to the plant has been depleted.) A 5,700-foot conveyor system solved the problem of getting the raw material from pit to plant. A belt 3 feet wide delivers 500 tons per hour of material finer than 5 inches in diameter. The system is in nine sections, or "flights," ranging in length from 120 to 2,005 feet, each powered by an electric motor. The system passes under the tollway bridge at the DuPage River. The entire line is covered, to protect the gravel from wind and rain and to help keep the belts in alignment; it has become known as "the big green snake" by CB radio users on the tollway. The belt system was chosen in preference to truck transportation. Though initial cost was about the same, trucks would have needed eight drivers, whereas the conveyor system needs only two maintenance men. Replacement costs also favored the belt system.

At one of the world's largest salt mines, 1,000 feet underground at Retsof in western New York, a belt-conveyor system was installed in 1974. It replaced 13 electric locomotives, 750 mine cars, and 40 miles of track. The belt system, 3½ feet wide and more than 3 miles long, provides smooth, even, quiet operation. More important, it

has reduced the costs of labor and electricity, and has increased production by 21 percent.

Two-way belt conveyors are in operation at a few places. At a phosphate-rock mine in Florida, the top strand of such a belt transports raw material from mine to processing plant, and the bottom strand takes waste sand back to the mine area where it is used in reclamation. The belt is 4½ feet wide and nearly 3 miles long, with a capacity of 6,000 tons per hour. Though more expensive to install than the customary slurry pipeline, the belt needs only about one-tenth the power, moves material in both directions, and, being independent of water supply, will remain running even during dry periods.

Long-distance overland belt conveyors are also in use. A 4-foot-wide belt in Morocco brings phosphate rock 62 miles from a deposit in the Sahara to a port on the Mediterranean. Unfortunately this line, with its 10 control stations, has

In business with belts. Conveyor belts move thousands of tons every day at this Florida plant, where phosphate rock is washed, screened, and stockpiled. (Courtesy of Florida Phosphate Council.)

The belt takes a beating. Crushed stone falls onto a moving conveyor. Empty "lower strand" of belt is out of view below. (Courtesy of National Limestone Institute.)

been under intermittent attack by Algerian guerillas. Belt conveyors, being on the surface and unattended for long distances, are open to sabotage and armed assault.

Belt conveyors of the conventional, long-used type have certain other disadvantages. Each flight must travel in a straight line. To change direction, one flight must discharge onto another with a different alignment. Furthermore, the length of any individual flight is limited by belt strength. In recent years, however, belt length and load-carrying ability have been greatly improved by giving the rubber belt a core of 3/8-inch steel cables, instead of rayon or nylon cord. The new belts deliver as much as 20,000 tons per hour and can be set up with flight lengths as great as 16,000 feet. Power is supplied at several places along the line instead of just at each end of the flight. These belts will withstand operation in a "deep-dish" cross section for increased loads. Curves are even possible, as in a 3,000-foot belt in Sweden used for loading ocean-going ships with cement. Belt conveyors are used worldwide in the coal and metal-mining fields, as well as in the nonmetallics, and there is little doubt that their use will increase.

On and Off the Highway

Movement of earth materials by truck is so commonplace that it requires little comment. Stone, sand, concrete, brick, and wallboard are regular

A surge pile. Belt on the left brings crude rock from the quarry; belt on the right reclaims it from beneath, as needed by the plant. The surge pile acts as a "cushion" between quarry supply and plant demand. This is at a perlite plant in New Mexico.

A bucket elevator. Gravel is being reclaimed from underwater storage in the harbor at Rotterdam, The Netherlands. The gravel was dredged from the sea bed of the English Channel.

travellers on the highway. Special adaptations are seen daily, like the ready-mix concrete truck with its slowly revolving drum, and the flatbed truck with its own mechanism for loading and unloading pallets of bricks or concrete blocks. Not all the tank trucks that we see contain liquid; some carry powdered material like lime or cement.

Less familiar are the "off-highway" trucks used in many pits and quarries. Being unrestricted as to weight or clearance, some of these machines are immense. In an open pit at Asbestos, Quebec, trucks with as much as 200 tons capacity carry rock from quarry face to primary crusher. (The average pick-up truck carries no more than one ton). The driver of one of these machines climbs to his cab by a ladder; the diameter of the front wheels exceeds the height of a man. Near Soda Springs, Idaho, phosphate rock is hauled from mine to plant by "truck trains" on a company-built road 15½ miles long. A truck train consists of a tractor unit pulling three trailers, each carrying 42 tons of rock. Each train is 165 feet long, and has 50 tires! Mine owners decided on trucks in preference to building a rail line, mainly on the basis of flexibility.

Indeed, versatility and flexibility—spot pickup and delivery—are the strong points of truck transport. On a cost-per-ton mile basis, however, it is five to ten times as expensive as rail haulage. After all, 50 highway tractors hauling 50 trailers means 50 engines consuming fuel and 50 drivers earning wages. The same 50 trailers on railroad flatcars can be hauled by one engine with a small crew.

Rocks by Rail

When many thousand tons of rock must be moved overland, train transport is often the answer. This is especially true if delivery must be made regularly, every day or every week. Heavy, bulky commodities can be moved by rail at a fraction of the cost of truck transport.

Special handling. To move a train of rock or sand down the line is simple: you attach an engine and pull. But this is only a part of the story. The cars have to be loaded at the point of origin and unloaded at the destination, and these processes must take up as little time as possible. A railroad car is not a storage facility: it is earning money

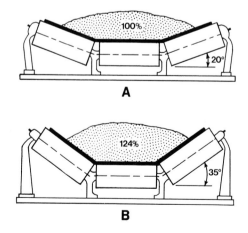

A. Cross section of a conventional conveyor belt (heavy black line) and its supporting rollers, or "idlers," with a typical load of gravel or stone. B. An increase in tilt of the idlers can greatly enlarge the capacity, but the belt must be very tough to withstand the additional bending. (Courtesy of Mining Engineering.*)*

Over-the-road trucks at an English kaolin plant. (Courtesy of English China Clays Group.)

only if it is out on the road hauling something. So a great deal of expensive equipment is devoted to reducing the time spent at either end of the line. In fact, railroads are as much in the "materials handling" business as in transportation.

In a recent year, 15 million tons of bulk cement was shipped by rail. Since this gray powder must be protected from wind and weather, it is carried in specially designed covered rail cars. Loading is generally through enclosed conduits by simple gravity flow. Unloading may also be done by gravity, to trucks or to conveyors that take it to storage, or pneumatically by a truck-mounted air compressor. Such a system moves 100 tons of cement via a dry pipeline to a storage silo, or to trucks, in less than an hour.

Near Windermere, in the spectacular Rocky Mountains of British Columbia, a quarry supplies gypsum for a wallboard plant. The plant, however, is not next door, but is at Vancouver, some 500 miles away. Every week, 20 covered rail cars, each carrying 100 tons of gypsum, leave the quarry for the plant, and are returned empty. The cars are gravity-loaded from elevated storage bins at the mine and discharge by gravity into a bin or hopper at the plant. The rail shipment thus serves as a wheeled conveyor, carrying 2,000 tons per week.

Under the right conditions, even such a lowly material as gravel for aggregate is moved by rail. A concern in Shreveport, Louisiana, obtains its material from a deposit in Arkansas, 135 miles away, in trains of nineteen 100-ton-capacity cars, on a 3-day turnaround basis. Processing and screening are done at the pit, so the material

Special delivery. Truck brings ready-mixed concrete to an airport construction site. (Courtesy of Portland Cement Association.)

shipped is ready for use in concrete when it arrives.

Shuttle trains. A special payoff in rail transportation comes when demand is sufficient to support one or more *unit trains*. A unit train consists of cars carrying only one commodity and moving between two points on a regular basis. Trains of 75 cars or more shuttle back and forth. The cars are quickly loaded and unloaded by means of extensive materials-handling equipment.

When a construction company in Denver found that its close-in sources of aggregate were becoming depleted, they turned to a deposit some 43 miles away near the town of Lyons. Here, on the Rocking WP cattle ranch, was 300 acres of gravel 10 to 20 feet thick. But how to move this material to the Denver plant? A study showed that a fleet of

30 trucks, running nine hours per day, would be needed to deliver the daily requirement of 3,000 tons. Costs of fuel and labor would be high. Fortunately, a railroad spur crossed the property. So the company bought 30 rail cars of 100 tons capacity each, and contracted with the railroad to move this train daily as a unit. The train does the job in only five hours and uses one-fifth the fuel that trucks would have required. It is picked up at the Denver yard every morning, hauled to the deposit, and loaded as it passes slowly beneath six silos. On return to Denver, the bottom-dump cars release their load onto a stockpile below a trestle. The train moves across the trestle at one mile per hour, and is unloaded in only 15 minutes.

Much longer hauls are not uncommon. For years, sulfur from the Calgary area of Alberta has been moved by unit train to tidewater at Vancouver for shipment overseas. (The sulfur is recovered as a by-product of natural gas high in hydrogen sulfide.) In 1980, unit trains started carrying potassium fertilizer from mines in southeastern Saskatchewan to terminals in Iowa and Illinois. This involved round trips of 1,600 to 2,000 miles. Trains of about 75 cars, belonging to Canadian rail lines, were loaded at Saskatchewan plants in 30 hours and unloaded at U.S. warehouses in 24 hours; round-trip time, 15 days. Because the soluble potassium compounds must be protected from the weather, covered hopper cars were used, and special storage facilities were built. The system is designed to assure delivery of fertilizers to the market area of the midwestern states. About 400,000 tons per year are handled.

A truck train hauling phosphate rock from mine to plant on a company road in Idaho. (Courtesy of Monsanto Company.)

Off-the-highway truck. Its capacity is 100 tons, or six buckets-full from the electric shovel. Trucks of this type are common in open-pit mines. (U.S. BORAX photograph.)

Waterborne Cargoes

The humble barge. A truck can haul about one-tenth of a ton per horsepower, a train about 1 ton. But a river boat with a "tow" of barges can move as much as 8 tons per horsepower. So, whenever a shipper of large-bulk low-value commodities has a choice between overland transpor-tation and water transportation he is likely to choose the latter.

Barges are widely used by those producers of aggregate that are fortunate enough to be situated on a waterway. Crushed stone produced at Haverstraw, New York, enters the lucrative New York City market, 35 miles away, because it can be moved cheaply by barge down the Hudson River.

Why shippers like the water. A truck moves much less than one ton per horsepower, a train about one ton, and a barge as much as eight tons.

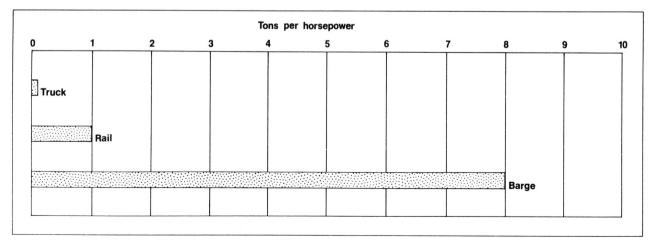

Salt is unloaded from a Mississippi River barge at Dubuque, Iowa. It will be used for de-icing streets and highways. The salt comes from a mine in a salt dome at Cote Blanche, Louisiana. (Courtesy of Domtar Industries Inc..)

Another large-bulk product that moves by barge is cement. Transporting this material is a somewhat more specialized operation, as the barges must be covered, sealed against the weather, and kept free of contaminants. In 1980, a cement company placed in service a new $5 million ocean-going barge. It transports 6,000-ton shipments from the company's manufacturing plant at Catskill, New York, to terminals in New York City, Boston, and Providence. The barge is 300 feet long and 60 feet wide; its stern is notched to accommodate the tug with which it is moved and maneuvered. The vessel carries its own unloading equipment and requires a crew of only two men.

Other special-purpose barges are in use, for example, those with thermal insulation for carrying molten sulfur.

At several European ports, barges act as transit vessels, taking cargo from ocean-going ships to dockside destinations, often on a river far from the sea. Many of the picturesque Rhine barges are performing this duty.

OBOs and company ships. Owing in large part to the insatiable demands of the industrialized nations for raw materials, many rocks and minerals enter overseas trade. But they can hardly be said to dominate it. The maritime freight market for dry cargo (as opposed to crude oil) is governed by the "big three": grain, coal, and iron ore. These move in superships of 150,000 tons capacity or more. The only nonmetallic that approaches them in size of shipment is phosphate rock, used in the manufacture of fertilizer. About 5 percent of the trade in this commodity is done in vessels of more than

50,000 tons, especially in oil/bulk/ore (OBO) carriers, for example, in the haul from Florida to the Arabian Gulf region. Another 15 percent is carried in ships of 35,000 to 50,000 tons capacity, from Morocco, the world's largest producer of phosphate rock, to western Europe, which consumes over half the world production.

The largest tonnage of industrial rocks and minerals moves in ships of no more than 30,000 tons capacity, most of which belong to mining companies. For example, gypsum is carried from quarries on San Marcos Island, on the west coast of Mexico, to wallboard plants in California, in company-owned ocean-going ships. One load of 26,000 tons keeps a plant supplied for more than a month. Similar ships bring gypsum from Nova Scotia to plants on the east coast. These ships have automatic self-unloading systems, which deliver 2,000 tons per hour and minimize turn-around time in port. Here as elsewhere, efficient handling of materials helps make operations profitable.

Cement is another large-bulk material that enters the sea lanes. Most of the traffic is in coastal vessels, averaging only about 4,000 tons capacity, but at least a dozen ocean-going ships each carry more than 20,000 tons. In 1978, the United States imported about 8 percent of its net consumption of cement, or some 7,000,000 tons. Large suppliers were Norway, Spain, the United Kingdom, and France. International trade in cement is hampered because there is no universally accepted materials-handling system, either on the ships or at ports.

Tramps. Much industrial-minerals traffic is in consignments of only a few thousand or even a few hundred tons—far too small to fill the average freighter. So they go as "part cargoes," generally in the unscheduled vessels known as *tramps*, which pick up and deliver cargoes wherever and

Gypsum arrives at this Mexican port via unit train at left. From the stockpile it moves by belt to the ocean-going ship. The gypsum will be used in the manufacture of wallboard at a California plant. (Courtesy of United States Gypsum Company.)

whenever these can be found. Shipments may be in bulk, for example, several thousand tons of crude barite from Foynes, Ireland, to New Orleans, to be ground up for use in oil-well drilling. Products that have already been processed for the consumer are likely to be shipped in packaged form, for ease in handling and protection against contamination. High-grade white kaolin clay for paper-making, for example, may be shipped in 50- or 100-pound bags, stacked on pallets, each pallet-load being shrink-wrapped in heavy plastic. Other commodities may go in standard shipboard containers, each with a plastic liner, or in re-usable flexible containers of woven propylene cloth with cord or wire reinforcement. In 1978, an exceptionally large shipment of paper clay—16,000 tons in bagged form—left Savannah, Georgia, for Japan.

Travelling on a tramp steamer of 25,000 tons capacity, it included consignments to five different Japanese ports.

Ships also carry kaolin in slurry form—about 70 percent solids. Slurry shipment reduces labor and equipment costs, and provides the customer with a clean, dust-free product in a form ready for use. Coastal shipping of various mineral products in European waters is increasingly done in "mini-bulkers," ships of modern design that carry 2,500 to 3,500 tons. In spite of these specialized developments, however, the industrial minerals, in the words of a shipping expert, "are likely to continue to be overwhelmingly dependent for their transportation to distant markets on that remarkably versatile and obliging beast of burden, the tramp ocean freighter."

Small vessels load kaolin at a port in Cornwall, England, for coastal and cross-channel delivery. (Courtesy of English China Clays Group.)

Total Transportation

A system that integrates several techniques has been developed by a company that manufactures mineral fertilizers. Phosphate rock, mined in central Florida, travels 40 miles by unit train to Tampa. There the rail cars are automatically positioned and dump the rock into a 26,000-ton barge. This makes a 450-mile trip across the Gulf of Mexico and up the Mississippi River to the company's phosphoric-acid plant. The self-unloading barge discharges the rock at a rate of 3,000 tons per hour to a conveyor system at dockside, which takes it to storage piles. A reclaiming system provides the feed for the plant.

Such a system is simple to set up and maintain, because the entire operation belongs to one company and no material changes ownership. The pic-ture is different when a producing company sells to a consumer, especially if the consumer is several thousand miles away. The conventional procedure is to load the consignment on a tramp vessel and assume its safe arrival. If there are several customers, even though located close together, each must have its own consignment. Packaging is expensive and packaged shipments are subject to high freight rates. Today it is increasingly common for the seller to control the entire flow, from mine or quarry to point of consumption, much as an oil company controls its product from oil well to gas station. In this way the seller can be sure that his product goes at the lowest freight rates, is not damaged or contaminated en route, and arrives in the form desired by the consumer.

Kaolin moves from truck via covered belt conveyor to small freighter.
(Courtesy of English China Clays Group.)

An interesting example of "total transportation" is provided by trade in the industrial mineral borax (hydrous sodium borate). This is a clear to white mineral, of value in glass, enamel, detergents, and other products. First mined 100 years ago from the bed of a dried-up lake in Death Valley, California, borax was moved 165 miles to the railroad at Mojave in wagons pulled by mules. The 20-mule team became a legend of Death Valley and a famous trademark. Today, the chief production is from a deposit about 100 miles to the south, which fortunately is situated on a railroad line. Most of the free world's supply of borax comes from this single deposit, which supplies a strong overseas market, especially in Europe. In the 1960s the producing company decided to switch from shipping in bags, at a freight rate of as much as $30 per ton, to shipping in bulk at a fraction of that figure, and to maintain control of the entire operation. Several major changes were required by that simple decision. A bulk terminal had to be constructed at tidewater in Los Angeles to receive the borax from the mine and store it in silos. Another bulk terminal was built in Rotterdam, with facilities for unloading, bagging, storing, and trans-shipping the borax to European customers by ship, barge, rail, or truck. As for ocean transportation, an ingenious contract was worked out with a German manufacturer of automobiles. A specially modified ship brought cars to Los Angeles and returned with bulk borax to Europe. Obviously this arrangement was economical, as the ship was loaded on both trips and there was no empty "back-haul." The contract was in effect for 13 years, being discontinued only when declining sales of the imported cars on the west coast no longer allowed guarantee of adequate vessel schedule. Today, the borax is moved under contract with a Japanese shipping company without the regular back-haul of former times.

An ingenious proposal would provide cement raw materials to developing countries that export crude oil. Under this plan, a slurry of properly blended cement raw materials, with a chemical additive to keep them in suspension, is pumped aboard an oil tanker at a U.S. port. The ship delivers the slurry to a developing country for manufacture into cement. (For countries that are short of the needed facilities, a complete cement-manufacturing plant, mounted on two connected 200,000-ton tankers, has been proposed). After delivering its shipment, the tanker returns with a load of crude oil. Proponents of the plan state that no cleaning would be required at either end. Economic advantage, of course, is that both voyages are made with the ship fully loaded.

Whether crushed stone is to be moved across a quarry floor or borax across the sea, it is clear that transportation is a central and challenging part of the industrial-minerals picture.

3.

The Disassembly Line: Taking Rocks Apart

Nearly all rocks are mixtures of minerals, sometimes of two or three, often half a dozen or more. One mineral may predominate, as calcite does in limestone, but commonly several minerals are present in sizable percentages. Granite, for example, the most abundant rock in the continental parts of the earth's crust, consists of roughly one-third quartz, up to 15 percent black mica and other dark minerals, and the remainder a couple of varieties of feldspar—plus trace amounts of two or three other minerals. Even the one-mineral sedimentary rocks, which are so rare and valuable that they get special attention in Chapter 4, are hardly ever really pure; a few percent of other mineral matter is practically always present.

It commonly happens that one of the minerals in a rock is useful but the others are not. The question then arises, how do we separate the desired mineral from its associates? In this chapter we look at some examples of this challenging, complex, and altogether fascinating aspect of our stone-age culture.

Sink or Float

At a quarry in northern Ohio, rock is blasted down, crushed, and taken to a plant for processing. The material quarried is a sedimentary rock that consists of about 60 percent shale (consolidated clay or mud) and 40 percent gypsum (hydrous calcium sulfate, $CaSO_4 \cdot 2H_2O$). The gypsum is the desired material. As we saw in Chapter 1, it is used in the manufacture of plaster and wallboard. The word comes from the Greek *gypsos*, white plaster.

The gypsum is bright white. It occurs as thin layers, as egg-size to potato-size masses, and as contorted larger bodies, all separated by, or enclosed in, layers of brownish gray shale. Somehow the two must be separated. A hundred years ago, this might have been done the hard way—by hand. From the crushed rock as it passed by on a belt, workers would pick out and toss into a bin the white pieces of gypsum, along with those pieces that were mostly white and had only a little shale adhering to them. Today this procedure would be too expensive and too slow and would also be considered inhumane. (Eight hours at a picking belt can be classified as hard labor.) Leaping forward in time to the present hour of techno-

Wall of a gypsum quarry, northwestern Ohio. The white beds and masses are gypsum, the darker material shale. The two are separated on the basis of specific gravity. Hammer handle at left gives scale.

logical marvels, we might purchase an optical-scanning unit. Using the same property of the gypsum that the hand-pickers used, namely its white color, this machine would electro-optically identify pieces of gypsum and eject them from the stream of crushed rock by a precisely controlled air blast. But this technique is better suited to small volumes of material than to several thousand tons per day. It is also expensive to buy and install, and it requires feed that has been crushed to about one-half inch in size, further adding to the expense. So we are forced to look further.

The answer, it turns out, is simple. The gypsum has a specific gravity of 2.31 (that is, a given volume weighs 2.31 times as much as an equal volume of water); whereas the associated shale is heavier, having a specific gravity of about 2.8. We can utilize this difference very handily. The quarried rock, crushed to walnut-sized to fist-sized chunks, is fed into a big steel drum partly filled with a liquid having a specific gravity of 2.47. In this

liquid the gypsum floats and the shale sinks; it is an easy matter to withdraw them separately. The liquid is a water suspension of a gray powder called *ferrosilicon*, manufactured from iron ore and silica sand. The specific gravity of the liquid can be closely controlled. The ferrosilicon is reclaimed magnetically after it is washed off the gypsum and shale. So sink-float is the answer. Since ferrosilicon (and magnetite, which is sometimes used instead) are heavy media, a more commonly used term for the process is *heavy-media separation*, or HMS.

No doubt it has occurred to you that simply crushing the rock won't make a clean separation between gypsum and shale; some pieces will contain both. Quite true. As it happens, however, this presents no problem, as a little impurity in the gypsum doesn't affect its properties as plaster in wallboard. By the HMS process, we are able to upgrade 40 percent raw material in the quarry to 90 plus percent material for the manufacturing process.

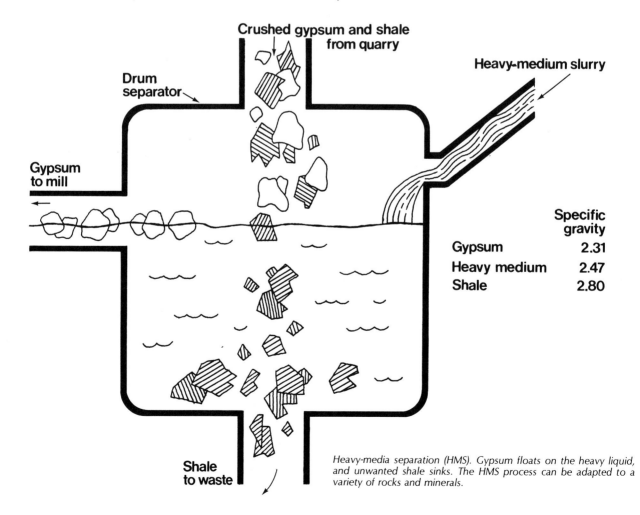

	Specific gravity
Gypsum	2.31
Heavy medium	2.47
Shale	2.80

Heavy-media separation (HMS). Gypsum floats on the heavy liquid, and unwanted shale sinks. The HMS process can be adapted to a variety of rocks and minerals.

High-purity gypsum at a quarry in Mexico. Material like this needs no preliminary treatment other than crushing and grinding. (Courtesy of United States Gypsum Company.)

Stone and Fiber

The word *asbestos* has been applied since ancient Greek times to any mineral that is composed of strong flexible fibers. Long-fiber varieties, which are up to 2 or 3 inches in length and are quite rare, can be combined with cotton or rayon and spun into thread and woven into cloth. This goes into such items as fireproof safety clothing and theater curtains. The much more abundant short-fiber asbestos (less than three-eighths inch) is used in floor tile, asbestos-cement pipe and paneling, brake linings, paper products, textiles, and a variety of other products.

About 94 percent of the world's production of asbestos is a mineral called *chrysotile* (a hydrous magnesium silicate). The most important deposits of this mineral in the free world are found in the province of Quebec, Canada, south of Quebec City and northeast of Montreal. Here, in a range of low hills, are masses of a dark greenish-gray rock called serpentinite. These masses are several thousand feet in width and length and extend to depths of hundreds of feet. Distributed throughout the bodies of serpentinite are innumerable veinlets of chrysotile, which average 3 to 5 feet in length and width but are seldom thicker than half an inch. They may be compared to extremely thin pancakes with tapering edges. Each is tightly packed with chrysotile. Most commonly the mineral occurs as "cross fiber," in which the fibers extend from wall to wall of the veinlet. Less common is "slip fiber," in which the strands are more or less parallel to the walls. When broken from the veinlet, the chrysotile is yellowish green (the word is from the Greek *chryso*, yellow, and *tilos*, fiber), but when disaggregated, or "fiberized," it makes a fluffy white mass like cotton. Each fiber is in fact a crystal; photographs made with the electron microscope show that the fibers are tubular in structure.

So here we have big masses of worthless serpentinite, shot through with veinlets of highly valuable chrysotile. How do we get the fiber out of the enclosing rock?

We are faced with an unusual circumstance at the start: chrysotile is merely a fibrous variety of serpentine, the mineral that makes up the host rock. Thus, veinlets and rock have the same chemical composition and the same specific gravity. About all we have to go on is the obvious difference in physical form—fibrous vs. stony—and it turns out that this can be made to do the job. The serpentinite, with its veinlets, is first mined in bulk, generally in a big open pit. At the mill it is dried and crushed. Fortunately, the walls of the veinlets are smooth, and crushing tends to free the fiber. When the crushed material is passed over vibrating screens, the particles of solid rock make a lower layer and the loose fibers make a layer on top. The fiber is then whisked off the screens by air suction, on the same principle as that of a vacuum cleaner. The cycle of crushing, screening, and air flotation is repeated until nothing is left on the screens but nonfibrous rock, which goes to waste disposal.

Asbestos ore. The desired fibers of chrysotile asbestos are in the light-colored veinlets; all the rest is waste.

Maximum recovery and minimum breakage of fiber are the objectives. For certain uses, the fiber is opened or fluffed out in special machines. All fiber undergoes a series of cleaning operations, designed to remove sand and dust, and is then classified as to length for marketing.

At one of the largest mines in Quebec, 39 million tons of rock is mined each year. Of this, 8 million tons is ore (serpentinite with asbestos veinlets) and about 625,000 tons is asbestos fiber. As you would expect, large amounts of air are required in separating the fiber. The average consumption at Canadian mills is more than 500,000 cubic feet of air per minute. As we will note in more detail in Chapter 8, chrysotile fibers may be harmful when inhaled over a long period of time. Dust collectors are integral parts of the milling circuit, the air in the mill is crystal-clear, and all air discharged from the mill is filtered.

So, to our list of agents that help to disassemble rocks, we may add simply: free air.

The Mineral That Melts

Some 35,000 to 40,000 feet below the flat coastal plain of southern Louisiana lies a thick bed of rock salt. It is buried beneath layers of sand and clay that have accumulated as the region slowly sank and the Mississippi and other rivers poured sand and mud from the continental interior into the sea. The salt bed lies below the reach of drilling, and we might not know anything about it if the salt had behaved like most sedimentary rocks and just continued to lie there. But salt, a one-mineral rock made up of halite (sodium chloride, NaCl), is a weak crystalline solid, and flows readily when stressed within the earth's crust. It flows in solid form, like ice in a glacier. Stress conditions favorable for such flow were set up in the Gulf

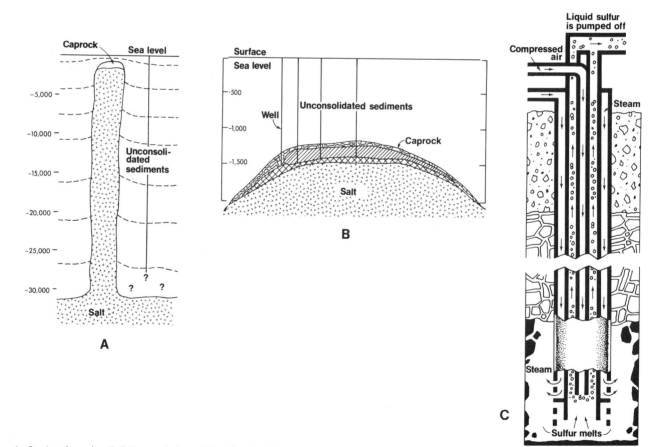

A. Section through a Gulf Coast salt dome. The pillar of salt has risen through some 30,000 feet of sand and clay because the salt is lighter than those sediments. B. Enlarged section through the caprock of a salt dome. Sulfur, if present, is found in a middle zone of impure limestone. C. Section through the lower part of a well that produces sulfur. Steam melts the sulfur, and compressed air helps lift it to the surface.

Coast region, because the sediments overlying the deeply buried salt are heavier than it is. This state of affairs made the salt unstable, giving it a certain buoyancy. Apparently, bulges or initial irregularities on the upper surface of the salt layer finally gave way, and pillars or columns of salt moved upward, through the beds of sand and clay, toward the surface. More than 225 of these salt columns are known in the Louisiana-Texas part of the Gulf Coast. In area they range from 100 acres to several square miles; the average is less than one square mile. They are commonly referred to as "salt domes," because they tend to arch or dome the sedimentary layers above them, not because they are domelike themselves. At about 150 domes, the top of the salt column lies at a depth of less than 3,000 feet—meaning that the salt in these columns has risen more than 30,000 feet from its parent bed.

Lying directly on the salt of most domes is a "caprock," which consists of anhydrite (calcium sulfate, $CaSO_4$), overlain by gypsum and impure limestone. Thickness of the caprock ranges from a few feet to 1,000 feet or more.

Taken as a group, salt domes are threefold mineral resources. Much oil and gas occurs in porous sandstones around their flanks, in cavernous caprock limestone, and in domed overlying strata. Second, the rock salt itself is mined at several domes. Third, important deposits of sulfur are found in the impure limestone of the caprock. Sulfur, along with limestone, salt, and coal or oil, is a mainstay of the chemical industry and therefore in strong demand. It is obtained in a unique manner.

Bright yellow sulfur, an element that is found in nature as a mineral, occurs in granular masses and crystal aggregates in the caprock limestone of certain salt domes. In 1895, a German-born American, Herman Frasch, devised the method of recovery that is still in use. It is based on a simple fact: sulfur melts at 110°C (230°F), not far above the boiling point of water. In the Frasch process, water at about 163°C (325°F) is injected into the sulfur-bearing caprock through wells. As the hot water leaves the well bore, it percolates through the formation and transmits its heat to the rock and sulfur. When the sulfur reaches its melting point, it separates from the rock. Since its specific gravity is nearly twice that of water, the sulfur flows downward and accumulates at the bottom of the well. It is then raised to the surface through a pipe inside the water-injection casing, an air lift being provided by compressed air introduced through a still smaller pipe within the sulfur line. The sulfur reaches the surface as a dark liquid, 99.5 percent pure. It is fed into bins, where it cools and solidifies. Great monolithic blocks of bright yellow sulfur, 30 feet high and several hundred feet long, are built up. The material is broken by blasting or by power shovels and is loaded for shipment to point of use. At some places, the molten sulfur, as it comes from the wells, is piped into specially insulated barges for transport in liquid form.

A critical factor in Frasch mining is an adequate supply of water—as much as 10,000,000 gallons per day at the larger plants. Another problem is that, when a new deposit is to be developed, a large and expensive plant must be built on the site of the salt dome, whether this happens to be physically favorable or not. One plant had to be constructed on the soupy muds of the Mississippi Delta; at another, the offshore Grand Isle dome, a steel island was built to support the heating plant and other equipment, as well as living quarters for 250 men. Frasch sulfur is also produced from bedded underground deposits in west Texas; here the ground is stable.

By the Frasch process, a valuable mineral resource is produced in essentially pure form without even disturbing, let alone handling, the unwanted rock material with which it occurs. All mining and processing should be so simple and efficient!

Disassembling Alaskite

Three industrial minerals in demand are feldspar, mica, and quartz. Feldspar, the most important, is an aluminum-silicate mineral rich in potassium or sodium. (*Feld* is German for field; *spar* is an old Germanic term for any light-colored mineral that breaks with smooth surfaces). Feldspar is a principal constituent of china, ceramic tile, and porcelain, and is also used in special types of glass. The other two minerals are by-products of feldspar production. The mica of commerce is mainly the light-colored variety, muscovite. It is finely ground and is used mostly in paint, in which its tiny flakes overlap like shingles on a roof. Mica is also used as a dusting agent to keep materials like roll roofing from sticking together. Ground quartz—pure silica, SiO_2—is used in specialty glasses.

Alaskite at a mine in the Spruce Pine district, North Carolina. This granitic rock is disassembled to yield feldspar, mica, and quartz. (Courtesy of The Feldspar Corporation.)

The rock at Spruce Pine. The country's most important producer of feldspar and its by-products is situated in the Blue Ridge Mountains of western North Carolina. Named for the town of Spruce Pine, the district is about 10 miles wide and 25 miles long. Most of the bedrock is gneiss and schist of no particular interest, but at hundreds of places these rocks have been thrust aside or replaced by igneous intrusions of granitic rock rich in feldspar, mica, and quartz. The majority of the intrusions are sheetlike bodies, termed *pegmatites,* averaging perhaps a few tens of feet in width and several hundred feet in length and depth. A few pegmatites contain occasional crystals of beryl and other rare minerals, and the Spruce Pine district has long attracted mineral collectors. (Emerald and aquamarine are gem varieties of beryl.) Also in the district are large intrusive bodies, a mile or more on a side, of a light-colored granitic rock called *alaskite.* This rock doesn't interest collectors, but it is the source of the district's commercial minerals.

Alaskite is a granitic rock consisting of 65 percent feldspar, 25 percent quartz, and 10 percent muscovite ("white mica"). The remarkable thing about this rock is not what is in it but what is missing. Dark iron-bearing minerals such as biotite and garnet, which are common in granites, occur in alaskite only in trace amounts.

The three minerals of alaskite are intimately intergrown, crystals of one penetrating the others in a complex three-dimensional pattern. It would seem an impossible task to sort out and segregate these three minerals, yet it is done, by the thousands of tons, as a matter of routine.

Crush it and grind it. Unlike pegmatites, which used to be mined laboriously by "gopher-hole" methods, the alaskite is quarried in bulk in large open pits in the same manner as stone for aggregate. Rock from the quarry is then put through a *jaw crusher,* which consists of two steel plates facing each other, one fixed and the other with a forth-and-back motion. Following this is a screen, which allows fine material to go through and bypass the next crushing stage. Coarse material from the jaw crusher goes to a *gyratory crusher.* Here the fixed steel face is much like the inside of a large bottomless bucket, and the crushing unit is a steel cone centered within it. The cone is fixed at the top but eccentrically mounted at the bottom, so that when turned it gyrates, continually opening and closing the gap between it and the fixed face. From this crusher the alaskite emerges at about ¾-inch maximum size and is stockpiled.

The stockpile, or "surge pile" as it is commonly called, is an essential feature of all such operations, as it provides a constant supply for the plant. A quarry may be shut down simply by turning the switch on the power shovel, but a complex processing plant must keep running.

A gyratory crusher. The bell-shaped unit of heavy steel swings in a circle, crushing rock fragments against the enclosing steel walls.

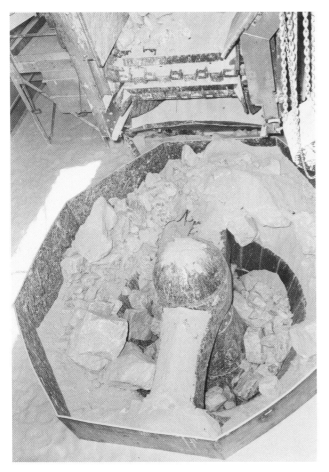

Top view of a gyratory crusher. Stone is crushed against the walls by the steel element below the dome-shaped support in the middle. (Courtesy of United States Gypsum Company.)

From the stockpile the rock is conveyed to a *rod mill*, a rotating horizontal steel cylinder several feet in diameter, in which the tumbling action of steel rods in the presence of water grinds up the material introduced. At some plants, a *ball mill* is included in the circuit. This is a rotating steel drum, tapered at both ends, in which the grinding is done by the falling and rolling action of steel balls. As feldspar for ceramic use must contain an absolute minimum of iron, the ball mill may be replaced by a *pebble mill*, in which the grinding is done by pebbles of quartzite, flint, or a nonferrous artificial material such as alumina or dense tough porcelain.

The bulk of the material that emerges from the grinding circuit is in the size range of 1.0 mm to 0.1 mm. At this level, separation of the three minerals is essentially complete. Further grinding would only use up energy and create "fines" to clog up the next stage of treatment. As it is, the grains smaller than 0.1 mm are discarded.

We note in passing that, although man has been grinding up rocks and minerals for centuries, there is still no generally accepted theory explaining why so much energy is needed, or what happens to the energy that is applied. As one expert concludes, the technique relies on "rules of thumb, technical expertise, and long years of experience" for converting hard rock from chunks into tiny grains at the lowest possible cost in energy.

Froth it and float it. The "mill feed," as the ground-up alaskite is now referred to, goes to a conditioning tank. Here it is agitated in water suspension, and a chemical reagent is added. This is a highly specialized organic compound, such as hydrogenated tallow amine, which will attach itself to the grains of mica but will ignore the grains of feldspar and quartz. The reagent imparts a water-repellent coating to the mica grains. In the next stage, a *flotation cell*, the feed is agitated further, and a frothing agent, such as pine oil or soap, is added. The mica adheres to the bubbles and rises with them to form a froth at the top of the cell. This froth is then skimmed off by paddles or simply overflows the top. It falls into a trough from which the mica is washed and reclaimed by filtering. The grains of feldspar and quartz, being readily wettable, do not attach themselves to the bubbles, and sink to the bottom of the cell. Sometimes wetting agents, or depressants, are added to further this action.

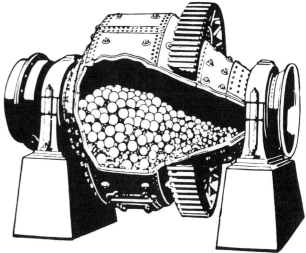

Cutaway view of a ball mill. Material introduced at left is reduced to a powder by the tumbling action of the balls as the mill rotates. Mills are six to eight feet or more in diameter.

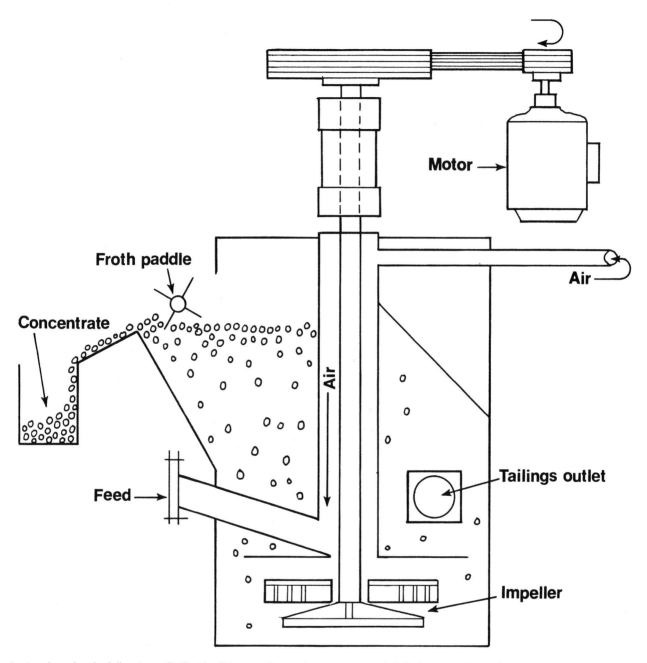

Section through a froth-flotation cell. The "feed" is ground-up rock plus a chemical that gives a water-repellent coating to grains of one mineral but not to others. Also introduced is a frothing agent, such as pine oil. The spinning agitator, or impeller, produces air bubbles, to which grains of the treated mineral cling. These bubbles rise and create a thick froth on top; this is skimmed off by rotating paddles. Unaffected grains sink and leave the cell. These cells range in size from about three feet on a side to more than six feet. Scores or hundreds are at work in large mills. (Courtesy of Industrial Minerals.)

The mica grains are floated off, washed, dried, ground, and bagged for shipment. The remaining mill feed then goes through a series of similar stages, a different reagent being added for flotation of each mineral. Iron-bearing minerals are floated and sent to the waste dump. Feldspar for glass manufacture is floated, washed, dried, and packaged; feldspar for ceramics goes through a high-intensity magnetic separator to remove the last traces of iron-bearing minerals, and is then ground very fine in a pebble mill before shipment. Finally, quartz for glassmaking is floated, dried, and bagged for shipment. Grains smaller than 0.1 mm are removed to waste all along the circuit.

The froth-flotation method converts the alaskite of Spruce Pine from just another rock to three valuable mineral commodities. Indeed, the method is adaptable to a variety of raw materials, for example, barite, used in oil-well drilling; fluorspar, for the chemical and metallurgical fields; and potassium minerals, for fertilizer. Besides being versatile, it is relatively inexpensive. And it makes separations that are, in the word of one qualified observer, "elegant."

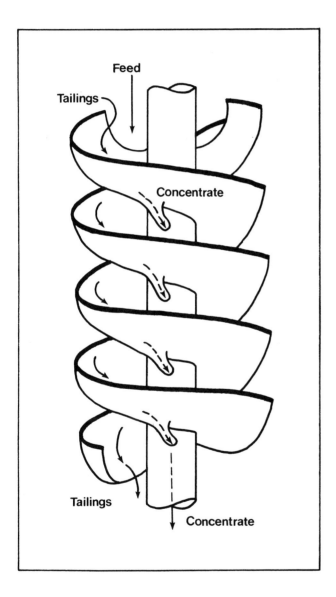

A spiral concentrator, used in processing heavy-mineral sands after the magnetic minerals have been removed. The feed is only 15 to 30 percent sand, the rest water. Under gravity, the light quartz grains stay on the outside of the turns, and the heavier grains of rutile and zircon move toward the axis. Capacity averages about one ton of sand per hour. Hundreds of these units are used at large plants.

A Business Built on Sand

Commercial quantities of several industrial minerals occur in certain beach sands. Deposits in the United States are found on the New Jersey coastal plain near Lakehurst and in north-central Florida. These deposits are not on present-day beaches, but are on older ones that have been abandoned by the sea as the land has risen. More important deposits are situated in Western Australia, 140 miles north of Perth, and on the eastern coast of South Africa, about 290 miles southeast of Johannesburg. The Australian deposit is 18 miles inland on an old upraised beach; the South African deposit consists of beach and dune sands right along the present shore line.

Like most sands, these deposits all consist mainly of quartz grains. What makes them valuable is their unusually high content of other minerals. These are chiefly *ilmenite* (iron-titanium oxide, $FeTiO_3$); *rutile* (titanium oxide, TiO_2); *zircon* (zirconium silicate, $ZrSiO_4$); and *magnetite* (iron oxide, Fe_3O_4). Because all these minerals have specific gravities well over 4.0, compared with 2.65 for quartz, they are commonly referred to as "heavy minerals." Ilmenite and rutile are converted (by different processes) into synthetic titanium oxide, a brilliant white pigment for paints. Zircon sand is used primarily as a molding sand to receive molten metal in foundries. Magnetite, if in sufficient quantities, is an ore of iron.

The proportion of heavy minerals in the sands mentioned ranges from about 4 percent to about 15 percent, averaging perhaps 5 percent. Considering the enormous tonnages of beach sands, even this low proportion means very large quantities of these minerals. How can they be obtained and concentrated?

At one operation, sand is extracted by a suction dredge in a pond excavated for the purpose. Since the raw material is already in the form of loose grains—that is, nature has done the crushing and grinding—there is no need for those processes. Floating alongside the dredge is a concentration plant, which separates the heavy minerals from the quartz. The key piece of equipment here is the *spiral separator*, which consists of an open trough in an inclined spiral. Sand and water are fed to the upper end, and, as the mixture passes rapidly down the spiral, the light quartz grains move to the

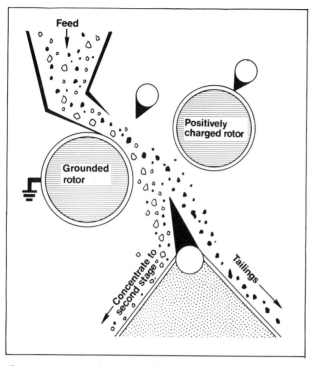

Feed

Positively charged rotor

Grounded rotor

Concentrate to second stage

Tailings

Electrostatic separation. Material to be sorted passes onto a grounded rotor. In the gap between this and a high-voltage electrode, particles become charged by electron flow, moving either toward or away from the charged rotor. In the set-up shown, the feed is diamond-bearing material. The diamonds, less conductive than the other minerals, fall directly downward. One "pass" seldom makes a complete separation, so a series of units is commonly used.

outside of the trough, leaving the heavy minerals on the inside. The two fractions are readily removed. An individual spiral concentrator is not a very large piece of equipment—about the height of a man and a couple of feet across—so a concentration plant may consist of as many as 1,500 of these units. The waste quartz sand is conveyed to the back of the pond, stacked, and revegetated. The dredge moves forward a few feet per day and stacks sand behind it at about the same rate; thus the pond advances along the beach.

The heavy minerals are pumped to a stockpile on shore. Magnetite is easily removed by passing the concentrate through a low-intensity magnetic separator; it goes to a stockpile. The next step is high-intensity magnetic separation, which takes out the ilmenite. It goes to a stockpile or to the plant that manufactures titanium-oxide pigment. The remaining rutile-zircon sand is dried and put through an *electrostatic separator,* in which the two minerals are given an electric charge and are deflected differently when brought into the field of an electrode. Rutile is retained. The zircon in the remaining sand is concentrated, dried, and passed

through a final magnetic separator. These two minerals go into storage for shipment.

Other Rocks, Other Methods

For certain uses it is necessary to achieve much finer grain size than is possible with even the best mechanical grinding equipment. In a *fluid-energy mill,* a finely ground mineral in a high-velocity stream of air encounters a similar opposing stream or a solid surface. Collisions between particles can reduce grain size to as little as one micron—one one-thousandth of a millimeter. One of the reasons why good-quality paint has such remarkable covering power and ease of application is that its pigments and other solids have been reduced to extreme fineness by treatment in a fluid-energy mill.

Optical sorting equipment separates rock fragments or mineral grains on the basis of color, reflectivity, fluorescence, or indeed any optical character that can be electronically sensed. Elements of such a machine are complex but the basic arrangement is not. Crushed or ground material is prepared by a feeding and presentation system. The moving particles are then scanned by a sensing system, which is essentially a photoelectric cell. Associated electronics decide whether each particle shall be accepted or rejected. If the latter, they activate a deflection device, generally a blast of air or water, that reacts in milliseconds to the sensor's decision. Accepted material passes in one direction, rejected material in another. Optical sorting equipment is widely used for concentrating barite, marble, talc, and many other industrial rocks and minerals.

Disassembling rocks that contain sodium, potassium, and boron, which are readily soluble, commonly requires *chemical processing.* The desired compounds are separated from unwanted associates by such processes as fractional crystallization, often under vacuum, and evaporation. It is even possible to take brines apart. At Searles Lake, a dry lake in the Mojave Desert of California, concentrated brine that saturates a body of salts underground is pumped up and processed to yield six important industrial chemicals. These, with their chief uses, are sodium carbonate (glass), sodium sulfate (paper), lithium carbonate (ceramics), potassium chloride (fertilizer), bromine (pharmaceuticals), and borax (glass).

4.

Pure Rocks, Naturally Refined

Roughly 100 chemical elements have been identified in the earth's crust. A few of these occur by themselves as "native elements," but most of them combine with others. Native elements, and naturally occurring combinations of elements, constitute *minerals*. We've already encountered several of these, including sulfur (S), calcite (calcium, carbon, oxygen: $CaCO_3$), and ilmenite (iron, titanium, oxygen: $FeTiO_3$). Although some 2,000 minerals have been identified, only two dozen or so are of prime significance in the formation of *rocks*.

We recognize a wide array of rock types, but they can be readily grouped into only three classes on the basis of origin. *Igneous* rocks include those, like lava and granite, that have resulted from the cooling and "freezing" of a molten fluid. *Sedimentary* rocks accumulated, mostly in the sea, as layers of sand, mud, sea shells, or precipitated salts. Examples are sandstone, shale, limestone, and gypsum. *Metamorphic* rocks have been formed from rocks of the other two classes by heat, pressure, and the action of hot waters within the crust. Marble (formed from limestone) and slate (from shale) are well-known types.

Most rocks, of whatever origin, are complex mixtures of minerals. As we saw in Chapter 3, disassembling a rock in order to separate a desired mineral from its unwanted associates is often complicated and always expensive. How nice it would be if we could find great quantities of a single valuable mineral, uncontaminated by others!

As it happens, just such one-mineral rocks have been formed at a few times in the earth's history. All are of sedimentary origin and occur in layered or stratified deposits. Because they can be used essentially as is and are measurable in billions of tons, these naturally refined rocks constitute mineral resources of great value.

Record of a Migrating Shoreline

One of the well-known mineral-producing districts of the midwestern United States is the vicinity of Ottawa, Illinois, about 75 miles southwest of Chicago. Here several companies produce high-purity quartz sand, mainly for the glass industry. The sand is obtained from a layer of sandstone that constitutes the bedrock below loose soil and river deposits. This rock differs from most sandstones in two respects: it is soft and easily extracted, and—much more important—it is exceptionally pure. Sand as it comes from the quarry is more than 97 percent quartz grains, which means 97 percent silica, SiO_2. Most of the remaining 3 percent is clay, which is readily removed by washing. Washed sand runs as high as 99.9 percent silica. It is light gray to white, and remarkably uniform in size of grains. For many years "Ottawa sand" has set the industry standard for high-silica raw material.

The deposit from which the sand comes is a widespread sedimentary unit known as the St. Peter sandstone. It is named from the town of St. Peter in southern Minnesota, where it is well exposed. Viewed regionally, the sandstone is in the form of a thin sheet, sandwiched between older sedimentary rocks below and younger ones above. It crops out at the surface of the ground only along its edges in Minnesota, Wisconsin, Iowa, and northern Illinois. It is also exposed in Missouri, notably at Crystal City some 30 miles south of St. Louis, where the sand is used in the manufacture of plate glass. To the east and south, from Iowa across Illinois into Indiana, the sandstone is buried by younger strata, but it can be recognized in cores from deep wells. In this large region—some 225,000 square miles—the St. Peter sandstone has an average thickness of 75 feet. In

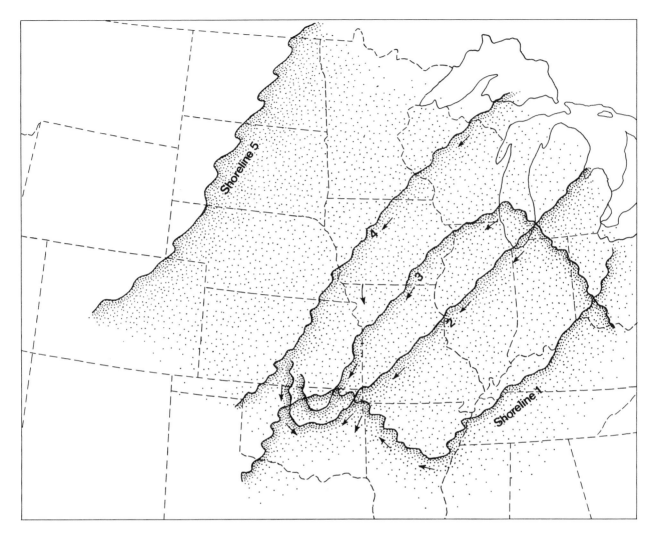

Beach sand to sandstone. In the early part of Middle Ordovician time, about 475 million years ago, eastern North America was gradually flooded by a shallow sea, which moved toward the northwest (shorelines 1 to 5). Aided by currents that brought sand from the northeast (arrows), the sea spread a thin sheet of quartz sand across the region. This sheet became the St. Peter sandstone of today—a pure and practically limitless deposit of silica sand. (Courtesy of American Association of Petroleum Geologists.)

this one sedimentary unit there are some 2,500 *cubic miles* of rock, nearly all of which is quartz.

The St. Peter sandstone is an unusual rock unit and records an interesting history. Fossils date its age as Middle Ordovician—which is geologese for about 475 million years ago. If you think about this figure for a moment, you will realize that, in discussing the geologic past, we move into a different time warp from everyday usage. Time in the geologic sense stretches back for more than 4 billion years! By the same token, we must erase our mental picture of today's geography, because the earth's surface was entirely different at remote times in the geologic past. Regional geologic studies tell us that in Middle Ordovician time

eastern North America was a featureless lowland, quite devoid of Appalachian Mountains. As this was long before the appearance of land plants on the earth, the lowland was barren of vegetation. It was bordered by a sea in the same relative position that the Atlantic Ocean has today. The land gradually sank, at perhaps a few inches or a foot per century, so that the sea advanced slowly across it. Like seas today, this one had a sandy beach, which was replenished by streams bringing sediment from the continental interior. As the sea slowly moved landward, it brought the sandy beach with it, leaving behind on the shallow sea floor a sheet of coalesced and submerged earlier beaches. Over a period of a hundred thousand

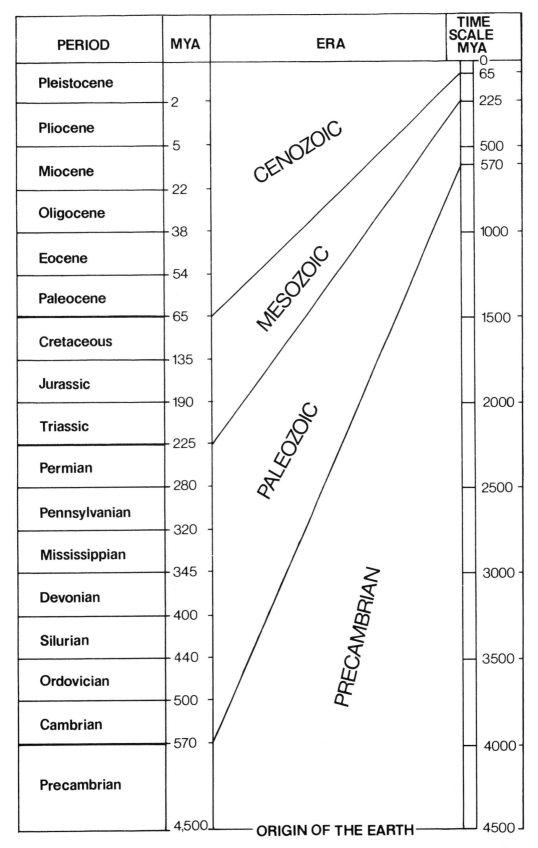

PERIOD	MYA	ERA	TIME SCALE MYA
Pleistocene		CENOZOIC	0
	2		65
Pliocene			225
	5		
Miocene			500
	22		570
Oligocene			
	38		1000
Eocene		MESOZOIC	
	54		
Paleocene			1500
	65		
Cretaceous			
	135		
Jurassic			2000
	190		
Triassic		PALEOZOIC	
	225		2500
Permian			
	280		
Pennsylvanian			
	320		3000
Mississippian			
	345		
Devonian		PRECAMBRIAN	
	400		3500
Silurian			
	440		
Ordovician			
	500		4000
Cambrian			
	570		
Precambrian			
	4,500	ORIGIN OF THE EARTH	4500

The major divisions of geologic time. MYA stands for "million years ago." The true scale on the right shows that about four-fifths of geologic time is Precambrian. Rocks rich in fossils are Paleozoic and younger.

years or so (a brief interval by geologic standards) the sea advanced into the east-central part of the continent. The St. Peter sandstone that we recognize today is the thin sheet of Middle Ordovician sand laid down in this shallow sea, largely covered by younger sediments that were deposited on top of it. As the geologist would put it, the St. Peter sandstone "represents the record of a shallow sea transgressing a stable continental platform."

There are a few other high-silica sandstones in this country, notably in Pennsylvania, Oklahoma, and California. All are of commercial value, and all have much the same sort of history as the St. Peter. Thus, the seemingly aimless and unfocused work of waves along a slowly advancing shoreline can

refine immense amounts of quartz sand to a high degree of purity. And, because nature did this refining, man doesn't have to. The almost limitless stores of pure silica are there for the taking.

Legacy of Coral Seas

To reconstruct in our minds the mode of origin of pure quartz sandstone, as just described, we must imagine a landscape utterly unlike that of today and a sea that took 100,000 years to produce a deposit of sand. We have no modern example of such a sea, and, even if we had, we could scarcely wait around for a thousand centuries to see the deposit made. But no such problems face us in envisioning the origin of high-purity limestone—

St. Peter sandstone in a quarry at Ottawa, Illinois. More than 97 percent consists of quartz grains, loosely held together by films of clay.

The rock is easily washed down by hydraulic jets. (Illinois State Geological Survey.)

A high-purity limestone, with abundant fossil shells and imprints. This rock accumulated in Florida in Miocene time, about 15 million years ago.

the premium grade of the versatile rock described in Chapter 1. This rock is rich in the remains of marine animals. Indeed, most pure limestone consists of little else but fossil shells and their broken fragments and ground-up paste. So the rock tells its own story. We know that we are looking at the record of teeming organisms that lived on the floor of an ancient sea. That the sea was clear is shown by the absence of mud or sand. The waters were undoubtedly warm, too, as are the modern seas that support corals and other invertebrate animals. Ancient invertebrates, like those of today, built their shells and skeletons of calcium carbonate. Thus, the rock formed by their remains is almost wholly this material in the form of the mineral calcite.

Shallow clear warm seas were widespread in central North America at several times in the geologic past, notably during the Middle Devonian, about 375 million years ago. Among the limestones that Middle Devonian seas left behind is a unit known as the Columbus limestone, named for exposures at Columbus, Ohio. The upper 40 feet of this 100-foot-thick bed of rock is 97 to 98 percent calcite. It extends from central Ohio to Lake Erie, and for some 50 miles eastward under cover of younger rocks. This upper part of the Columbus limestone is a highly valuable mineral resource, supporting several quarries and an underground mine.

The Columbus limestone contains a wealth of fossils. *Corals* include the type that grew in colonies, especially a large form with a surface sug-

gesting that of a honeycomb. Solitary "cup corals" or "horn corals" are also common. On the walls of quarries can be seen cross-sections of corals, and indeed of coral reefs, that grew in the Devonian sea. *Bryozoans*, or "moss animals," occur in twiglike or encrusting forms. They look something like miniature colonial corals. Also prominent are two groups of two-shelled, or bivalved, organisms. In the individuals of one group, the *brachiopods*, the two valves are different from each other, but each valve is bilaterally symmetrical. In the *pelecypods*, or clams, the two valves of each individual are alike but neither valve has bilateral symmetry. Likewise to be found are the coiled shells of *gastropods*, or sea snails, some with high spires and some with low. In the *cephalopods*, a single tapered shell is divided into compartments, as in the modern chambered Nautilus. Most of the cephalopod shells in the Columbus limestone are either straight or loosely coiled. With the corals, they may readily be seen in cross section on older buildings in which cut blocks of Columbus limestone were used for paneling, steps, or walls. Fragments of *trilobites*—distant relatives of the crab and lobster—can sometimes be found. Shelly remains of all the creatures we have named are embedded in mud made up of pulverized shell material; in places this mud has recrystallized to clear calcite. Coral reefs grew as mounds or banks on the sea floor. They were rigid, wave-resistant masses, which owed their rigidity to binding and encrusting marine plants, the calcite-secreting *algae.*

So invertebrate animals and certain marine algae were the humble agents that extracted calcium carbonate from the clear warm sea water. From time to time, storm waves ground up the shells, and currents spread the fragments over the sea floor. The general type of environment in which the Columbus limestone was deposited can be seen on the Bahama Banks in the warm Caribbean Sea of today.

Reefs of comparable purity, but different composition, are found in Silurian rocks of northern Ohio, Indiana, and Illinois. They are not now in their original form of calcite, but have been converted to a sister mineral, dolomite. This is calcium-magnesium carbonate. An unusually large quarry in one of these reefs is crossed by Interstate 80 at Thornton, Illinois, just south of Chicago. Pure

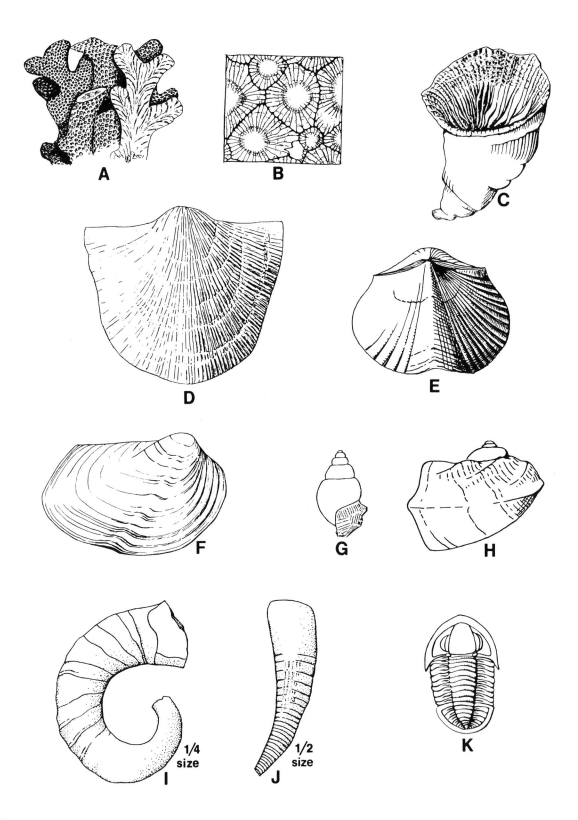

Common fossils of the Columbus limestone. These organisms lived in Devonian seas of what is now the east-central United States, about 375 million years ago. A. Fragment of a coral colony. B. Enlargement of A, showing sites in which individual coral animals lived. C. A solitary "horn" or "cup" coral. D and E. Brachiopods. F. A clam (pelecypod). G and H. Sea snails (gastropods). I and J. Cephalopods, early ancestors of today's chambered Nautilus. K. External skeleton of a trilobite, an extinct arthropod remotely related to crabs and lobsters. (Ohio Geological Survey.)

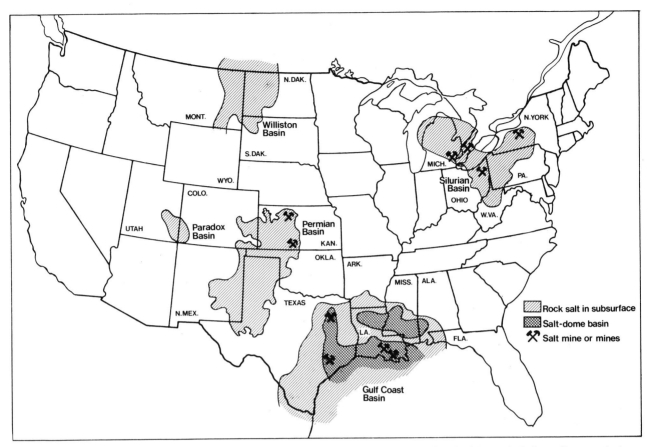

Major salt basins of the United States. The names Permian and Silurian indicate the geologic age of the salt-bearing strata. Salt deposits in the Williston Basin are Devonian, those of the Paradox Basin are Pennsylvanian, and the deep bed from which the Gulf Coast salt domes arose is Jurassic. (From a map in Handbook of World Salt Resources by S. J. Lefond. Courtesy of the author and Plenum Publishing Corp.)

dolomite rock from this quarry contains more than 98 percent carbonates (calcite plus dolomite). Such rock can be used for all the purposes of limestone except cement manufacture (its magnesium content rules it out for cement). In addition, it can be calcined to produce a magnesian lime, $CaO \cdot MgO$, which is highly resistant to heat and is therefore of value as a refractory material.

Salt of the Earth

Among the most useful of industrial minerals is rock salt, a white crystalline rock consisting of the single mineral halite (sodium chloride, $NaCl$). Besides being a food flavoring and preservative, salt is a basic chemical: its sodium and chlorine are used in scores of processes and products. Salt also keeps our roads and streets free of ice in the winter. It is used in water softening, textile manufacture, and many other applications.

Indeed, salt is not merely useful; it is essential to life. For this reason it has been sought and used since the dawn of history. From the salt mines of northern India to the shores of the Dead Sea, ancient lands were criss-crossed with trails made by salt caravans. References to salt abound in early literature, including the Bible. ("Can that which is unsavory be eaten without salt?") Many expressions referring to this substance have become part of our everyday speech. Those of Caesar's soldiers who were worth their salt received a part of their pay (their *salarium*) in that form. Since salt was a universal necessity and its source of supply could be controlled, it was an ideal substance for taxation—a fact that received rulers' attention from the earliest times. Smuggling, hijacking, and black-marketeering probably have ancient origins, in people's desire to escape a burdensome tax on salt.

Crystals of high-purity table salt, greatly enlarged, made by evaporating brine recovered in solution mining. (Courtesy of Morton Salt Division of MortonNorwich.)

Dissolve salt in water and you obtain a brine; evaporate the brine and the salt reappears as a white crystalline precipitate. Sea water, which contains 3.5 percent of salt, is the brine from which some commercial salt is produced, as we saw earlier: the brine is led into shallow broad ponds and allowed to evaporate, after which salt crystals are harvested. But less than 10 percent of our salt is obtained in this way. The rest is mined from underground deposits of rock salt. These are unusual, indeed unique, in several respects.

Most salt deposits accumulated in marine basins that were several hundred feet deep in their central part and occupied several thousand square miles. Thus, the salt beds are not thin sheets, but rather are deposits thick in the middle and thinning toward the edges of the ancient basin, like a lens in cross section. In Late Silurian time, a great salt basin extended from what is now western New York across Pennsylvania and Ohio into Michigan and Ontario; in the Middle Devonian, a basin existed in the North Dakota-Montana-Saskatchewan region; and in Late Permian time, about 230 million years ago, an extensive salt basin occupied what is now west Texas and southeastern New Mexico. The "mother salt" from which the Gulf Coast salt domes arose, as discussed in Chapter 3, is of Jurassic age, about 150 million years ago. Numerous other ancient salt basins, now evidenced by great lens-shaped salt deposits, are known in North America and other continents.

In humid-temperate climates, salt deposits are invariably underground. Salt is so soluble that near-surface beds are dissolved away in rain water, and the rock can exist only where it is protected from solution by overlying rocks. Mining is generally done by the room-and-pillar method, in which about half the salt is removed, the remainder being left in pillars to support the mine roof. Salt is also obtained by solution mining. Wells are drilled into the salt bed, and water is pumped down to dissolve the salt before returning to the surface. The "artificial brine" that results may then be evaporated to yield solid salt, or introduced directly into processes of chemical manufacture.

One of the most extensive salt mines in the western hemisphere, at Retsof in western New York, is developed in a bed of salt 18 feet thick at a depth of just over 1,000 feet. Salt is mined from beneath the city of Cleveland, at a depth of 1,770 feet, in a mine that extends out under Lake Erie. For many years, salt was produced from a mine about 1,140 feet below the city of Detroit. Several mines are active in central Kansas.

Salt is also mined at a few of the salt domes in the Gulf Coast. Since the salt here is not in a flat bed but in columns extending downward for thousands of feet, large caverns may be excavated in mining. In some of these, the ceiling is more than 100 feet above the level being worked. Mining has ceased at a few of these domes, and the cavities are now used for underground storage of crude oil.

In November 1980, an oil-company rig was drilling a well in Lake Peigneur at the Jefferson Island salt dome on the Louisiana coast. The lake, about 1 mile wide by 2 miles long, is at sea level; it fills a depression produced by solution of the underlying salt. On the southeast side of the lake was a salt mine, which had been active for many years. In the early morning of November 20, the drill apparently intersected this mine at a depth of about 1,400 feet. Within a few hours, lake waters and bottom mud poured into the mine, and the hurriedly abandoned rig disappeared into a collapse area on the lake bottom. Water was discovered early in the mine, and the mining crew was evacuated. No lives were lost in the entire sequence of events, but the oil company lost an expensive drilling rig and the salt company lost its whole mine. Lawyers for the two concerns are expected to be busy for a

Disaster at a salt dome. Upper photo: Lake Peigneur, a shallow lake at Jefferson Island, Louisiana. Shaft of salt mine is on promontory at left. Lower photo: Lake bottom after water had drained into salt mine.

Mine shaft is at A, mud flats at B, major collapse depression at C. (Courtesy of Joseph D. Martinez and Geotimes.)

A "salt saw," used to shear away large masses of salt in a mine at Belle
Isle, Louisiana. (Courtesy of Cargill, Inc.)

long time in an effort to fix responsibility. In the meantime, water from the Gulf of Mexico has re-filled the lake via a canal.

In sheer volume of deposits, rock salt exceeds all the other pure rocks. There are at least 3,000 cubic miles of salt in the Upper Silurian rocks of the New York-Ohio-Michigan basin, 10,000 cubic miles in the Upper Permian rocks of west Texas-New Mexico, and probably far more than that in the deeply buried salt basin of the Gulf Coast. Large parts of these enormous salt bodies are nearly pure, containing only 2 to 3 percent of impurities, chiefly clay and anhydrite (calcium sulfate).

The origin of these great deposits of salt has long been a puzzle and remains so today. The conventional view has been that the dominant process was evaporation. In this view, the sedimentary basin was shallow and acted as an immense salt pan under a sun so torrid that for long periods more water was lost to the air than flowed in via streams. Such a setting, however, would produce only a thin layer of salt, as in today's artificial salt-evaporating ponds. How to account for the scores of salt beds that are tens or hundreds of feet thick? It seems unlikely that the basin floor sank as fast as salt was added; evidence from other sources suggests that such accumulation was much more rapid than downward movement of the earth's crust. To meet this and other objections, it has recently been suggested that the salt may have been deposited from a layer of concentrated dense brine in a deep basin that did not dry up and was not a salt pan at all. But there are problems

Picking up salt. The two arms, in left corner and foreground, rotate in a scooping motion, gathering salt onto the belt at center which moves it back to a truck or conveyor. (Courtesy of Cargill, Inc.)

More than 30,000 tons of salt can be stored in this underground chamber at a Gulf Coast mine. Conveyors hoist the salt nearly 1,600 feet to the surface. (Courtesy of Cargill, Inc.)

with this concept too. The manner in which thick salt beds formed remains a geological enigma.

What Diatoms Did with Silica

In Santa Barbara County, California, about 12 miles inland from the Pacific Ocean, is a group of large quarries in a soft white rock called *diatomite*. These quarries are in the foothills of the Santa Ynez Mountains, near the town of Lompoc and the Vandenberg space-shuttle center.

Diatomite is a rock with exceptional properties, and these depend almost entirely on the way in which it was formed. In Miocene time, about 15 million years ago, the Lompoc region was covered by an arm of the sea. The waters were clear and shallow, and conditions were favorable for the growth of microscopic marine plants called *diatoms*. Each diatom consists of a minute speck of protoplasm—a single cell—enclosed within a shell or "test" of opaline silica (SiO_2 with a variable amount of chemically combined water). Most Miocene forms, like those of today, were floating organisms. When a diatom dies, its organic matter decomposes and is washed away, but its insoluble test of silica sinks to the bottom and accumulates with others of like origin. The resulting deposit is diatomite. In the Miocene waters of the Lompoc region, the growth environment was such that diatoms flourished by the billions over a long period of time, and several hundred feet of diatomite accumulated on the sea floor. Later uplifted and gently folded, these strata are now exposed in the "White Hills" and quarries near Lompoc.

A single cubic inch of diatomite may contain upwards of 40 million tests. Even more remarkable than sheer numbers is the incredibly complex structure and ornamentation of the tests. Members of some species have bilateral symmetry and look like boats, ladders, feathers, and needles. Others have radial symmetry and resemble wheels, discs,

Big rooms and big pillars in a mine at the Grand Saline salt dome, Texas. (Courtesy of Morton Salt Division of MortonNorwich.)

and golf balls. With the electron microscope we can produce images of the tests enlarged several thousand times, and such enlargement shows beautiful ornamentation and highly complex surface detail—ridges, spines, holes, dimples—down to dimensions of only 2 or 3 thousandths of a millimeter.

Because of their irregular shapes, diatom tests don't pack closely together. Contacts are limited mostly to the outer parts of each test, much as in a mass of loose thistledown. This means that the rock is extremely porous. From 40 to 60 percent consists of microscopic interconnected voids. In the ground, these voids are filled with water, so that after quarrying the rock must be dried. The air held in the tiny pore spaces after drying makes diatomite an efficient heat insulator. It also imparts light weight: a cubic foot of dry diatomite weighs only about 10 pounds, compared with more than 60 pounds for a cubic foot of water and 85 to 90 pounds for crushed limestone. Another property is enormous *surface area*. If we could iron out all the irregularities of all the tests in half a pound of

diatomite, we would obtain an area the size of a football field. No other substance, natural or artificial, has a comparable surface area. Diatomite typically contains about 90 percent silica, the remainder being mostly water of chemical combination and alumina from thin films of clay. This composition means that diatomite is insoluble in many chemical reagents. It is also resistant to heat, retaining its physical form up to about 1427°C (2600°F). This combination of properties is unique among earth materials.

Most diatomite is used in powdered form, either natural or calcined. Calcination, or heat treatment, shrinks and hardens the particles and unites some of them into microscopic clusters. But the structure of the individual diatom test remains the important feature of the material, on which almost all of its applications are based. Great care is taken in milling to preserve the particles' irregular shapes, spiny extensions, and intricately pitted surfaces.

A wide variety of uses has been found for diatomite. More than half is used in powdered form as a *filter aid*. Many liquids are difficult to filter, because the smaller particles pass with the liquid through the filter cloth or screen, whereas the larger ones remain on the filter and tend to clog it. To prevent this situation, pulverized diatomite is introduced in two steps. First, clear liquid containing a suspension of diatomite powder is passed through the filter until a coating composed entirely of this powder has been screened out on the filter cloth. Such a coating, 1/8-inch thick, presents about 2½ million capillary openings per square inch of surface. The second step is the addition of small amounts of the powder to the liquid to be filtered. As the turbid liquid reaches the filter, powder and impurities are caught. Continuous addition of a little powder to the liquid allows the buildup of a layer that constantly presents a fresh filtering surface. Diatomite filter aids are used in clarifying water, glucose, wine, syrup, antibiotics, oils, and solvents, as well as in swimming-pool filters.

Powdered diatomite is also used in paint. Not only is the powder useful because of its porosity, large bulk per unit weight, and ability to absorb oil, but it has a strong "flatting" effect. The angular diatom particles roughen the surface of the paint film, diffusing the light that strikes it, and producing a flat finish.

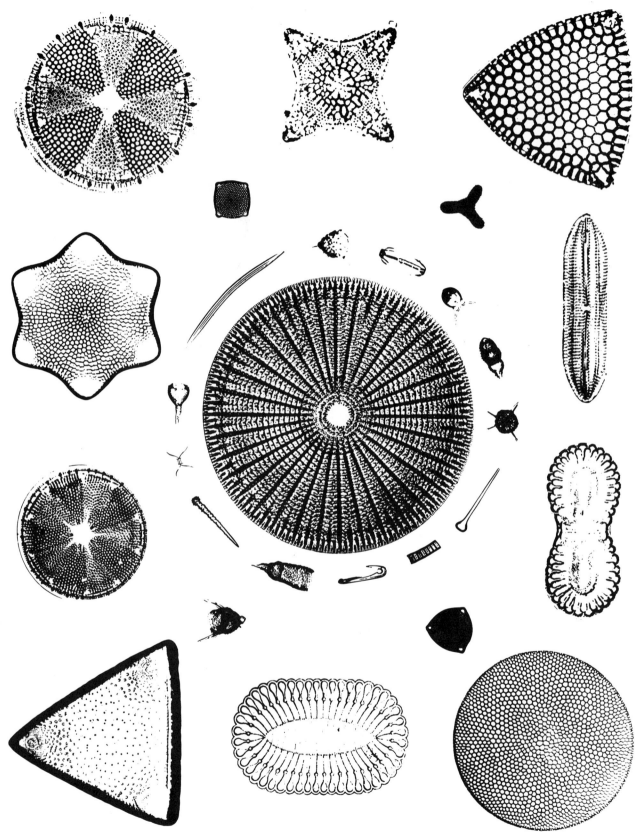

Some of the intricate tests, or shells, made by diatoms. The material is opaline silica. Greatly magnified. (Courtesy of Johns-Manville Sales Corporation.)

Diatomite is used as a filler, in such products as plastics and rubber; as a carrier of insecticides for spraying on crops; as an anti-caking agent in fertilizers; and in cement, composition roofing, plaster, and mild abrasives. The industry, which became established about 1900, has had an aggressive research and marketing policy, so that new uses for this versatile material are constantly being developed.

All deposits of diatomite are of Cenozoic age, which means they are relatively young (less than 65 million years). The material is mined in Mexico, Iceland, and several European countries. U.S. deposits are in California, Nevada, Oregon, and Washington. The Lompoc deposit, of marine origin, is by far the largest; other sizable deposits originated in fresh-water lakes. At all localities the diatomite is associated with volcanic ash and other evidences of volcanism. The silica used by the diatoms in building their myriad tests undoubtedly came to lakes or the sea in solution from volcanic hot springs or in streams that drained areas of silica-rich volcanic rocks.

Man applies much ingenuity to the selective quarrying of diatomite and to the production of many grades for sophisticated industrial uses. The fact remains that the value of this material rests on the strange and wonderful things that one-celled plants did with silica some millions of years ago.

"These Laboratories of Nature"

We have focused on the history of large deposits of single substances. This history has involved the washing action of waves in the shore zone, the work of corals and their associates on the sea floor, a sea evaporating under a scorching sun, and the raining-down of microscopic shells from surface waters onto the sea bottom. These processes are so diverse as to seem quite unrelated; yet they have at least four aspects in common. First, all are

Diatomite for filtration, magnified 500 times. (Courtesy of Johns-Manville Sales Corporation.)

sedimentary; none involves heat or pressure from within the earth. Second, all the processes take place through the medium of water, almost invariably the water of the sea. Third, all are quite usual processes: every one is going on today at some place on the earth (though not necessarily on the same scale as formerly). Finally, and of crucial importance, each process, once established, persisted for a long time: for hundreds of thousands, or even millions, of years. Hence, the exceptional size of the deposits we have discussed.

We find ourselves in agreement with W. H. Bradley, geologist and longtime student of the type of deposit we have described: "I confess that contemplation of these laboratories of nature where a complex dynamic system remains so long in apparent perfect balance fills me with something very close to childlike wonder."

5.

Five Chemical Minerals

Several nonmetallic minerals from the earth's crust are of great value for the elements that make them up—that is, for their chemical composition. In this chapter we look at five of these.

Sylvite

Sylvite is a flesh-pink mineral with the simple composition KCl—potassium chloride. It practically always occurs closely intergrown with another simple chloride, common salt (NaCl). Salt-sylvite beds are the relics of ancient seas that evaporated to almost complete dryness. Both minerals dissolve readily in near-surface waters, so commercial deposits are found only below a cover of younger rocks and must be mined underground.

Nearly all the production of sylvite, plus that of a few less important potassium minerals, is used in fertilizer. If you are a home gardener, you have encountered sylvite in packaged "NPK" fertilizer. This is a blend of compounds containing nitrogen, phosphorus, and potassium (K being the chemical symbol for potassium).

The name potassium is a Latinized form of an ancient workaday term, *potash*. This refers to the centuries-old practice of evaporating, in iron pots, solutions leached from wood ashes. The resulting "pot ash," potassium carbonate, was used in dyeing and tanning, and in making soap, matches, and other household needs. It was also known to be a useful plant food. Today, potassium content is given in terms of a sort of non-substance, potassium oxide (K_2O). This compound does not occur in nature, nor is it manufactured; it merely serves as a common denominator for the commercial comparison of all potassium compounds. Pure sylvite, for example, has a K_2O equivalent of 63

percent. "Potash" is now a general term, used in commerce, to apply to potassium minerals or compounds.

Up to the time of the Civil War, this country's needs for potassium fertilizer were met chiefly by the leaching of wood ashes. Development of large potassium-salt deposits in Germany began in 1861, and the United States shortly became entirely dependent on this source. But during World War I, Germany placed an embargo on exports, and the United States was forced to fall back on such materials as kelp, beet-sugar wastes, wood ashes, and saline-lake brines.

Although imports became available again after the war, it was obvious that this country needed domestic sources. This led to the development of deposits in southeastern New Mexico, where for years oil-company geologists had been reporting potassium-bearing minerals in well cuttings and cores. By 1931, commercial mining was established from below the desert plains east of Carlsbad, New Mexico. These deposits soon made the United States self-sufficient, and, in fact, an exporter of potash. Then, in the 1950s, immense deposits were discovered 3,000 feet beneath the plains of Saskatchewan, Canada. Though the Carlsbad district is still important, the focus of the industry has shifted to the larger and richer deposits north of the border.

Flat-lying beds of salt-plus-sylvite are relatively easily cut, and some of them can be mined by continuous-mining machines that bore big passages through the deposits. In the mill, sylvite is separated from the unwanted salt by grinding and by a sophisticated method of froth flotation, as described in Chapter 3. The resulting product is nearly pure potassium chloride. It is usable by

A continuous-mining machine, used in a potash deposit near Saskatoon, Saskatchewan, Canada. Bits at left rotate as the machine moves forward; broken rock passes through the machine and emerges at the back. (Courtesy of Saskatchewan Government Photos.)

Maintenance room 3,145 feet below the surface in a Saskatchewan potash mine. Walls show grooves left by continuous-mining machines. Entrance to mining area is at lower left. Mining crews travel on personnel carriers like the one at lower right. (Courtesy of Saskatchewan Government Photos.)

Trona, showing radial crystalline structure. (Courtesy of L. E. Mannion.)

plants to synthesize starch and sugar, promote root growth, and resist adverse conditions of

climate and disease. The bulk of the product goes to big farms and "agribusiness" concerns. It is shipped in unit trains of covered hopper cars and is handled at special weatherproof storage facilities.

Trona

Early in 1938, wildcatters drilling for oil on the plains of southwestern Wyoming struck a different kind of pay dirt. Between the depths of 1,590 and 1,600 feet, the drill penetrated a layer of *trona*. (The name is of Arabic origin.) This is a light-colored crystalline mineral, a hydrous sodium carbonate, $Na_3H(CO_3)_2 \cdot 2H_2O$. Long known to occur in dry lake beds, trona had never before been found in a sizable underground deposit. Though the well turned out to be a dry hole, the discovery of trona

Loading trona in a Wyoming mine. Arms on front scoop the ore onto a belt, which moves it back and into a vehicle for removal. Air duct for ventilation shows beyond machine. (Courtesy of Stauffer Chemical Company of Wyoming.)

was to have a marked effect on a major segment of the chemical industry.

Sodium carbonate, Na_2CO_3, known in the trade as *soda ash,* is a chemical of much industrial importance. It is one of the three substances from which glass is made. It is also used in making soap, detergents, water softeners, and paper—not to mention washing soda and baking soda. For more than 100 years, soda ash has been manufactured in a process devised by two Belgian brothers, Ernst and Alfred Solvay. In this process, a salt brine is saturated with ammonia, the ammoniated brine is carbonated with CO_2 from a lime kiln, and a sodium-bicarbonate slurry is formed. The bicarbonate is then filtered from the liquid.

The production of soda ash by the Solvay process was well established in all the industrialized nations, including the United States. The Wyoming discovery of trona changed the picture dramatically. In 1938, 17 Solvay-process plants were producing soda ash in this country; by 1969 the number had dropped to ten, and in 1979 there was only one left. Trona, the natural sodium carbonate from mines in the Green River Basin of Wyoming, had taken over. It was even being exported to Europe, to the consternation of the long-established Solvay industry there.

In the field of industrial minerals there are numerous examples of synthetic substances taking over world markets from natural ones. The soda-ash picture is a refreshing development in the opposite direction.

Exploratory drilling that followed the discovery showed the presence of enormous amounts of

In many room-and-pillar mines, like this trona mine in Wyoming, the roof is stabilized by bolting. Here the operator directs a machine that drills a hole upward. He will then insert a rod with an expander at the upper end and a plate at the lower. Turning the bolt fastens the roof securely to overlying strata. Rods awaiting use are on truck at left. Plates in the roof mark earlier bolts. (Courtesy of Stauffer Chemical Company of Wyoming.)

trona in the subsurface of southwestern Wyoming, at depths ranging from 400 to 3,500 feet. More than 40 beds have been found. Of these, 11 are more than 6 feet thick and are pure enough to be mined. The gross area involved is some 1,200 square miles. Commercial production started in 1946. In 1980 there were four companies mining trona, one from a bed at 800 feet and the others from a bed at 1,500 feet. The trona is refined in large plants by a series of complex chemical processes to produce pure sodium carbonate. Fortunately the district is crossed by the Union Pacific Railroad so that transportation is assured.

The trona accumulated in flat-lying beds in a large lake of Eocene age (some 50 million years ago). This lake occupied a broad shallow depression in what is now called the Green River Basin. Layers of ordinary shale, oil shale, freshwater limestone, and volcanic ash also formed. Some of the trona is intergrown with salt, and it is probable that the trona is a product of the evaporation of lake waters. An interesting geologic question arises in this connection. The Green River Basin is one of about 10 similar basins in the Rocky Mountain region, but only one other basin contains sodium salts, and these in far smaller quantities. Why did 50 billion tons of sodium carbonate accumulate in the Green River Basin but not in the others? The answer seems to lie in volcanic action. Some sodium was undoubtedly contributed by volcanic ash that fell into the lake. Streams draining adjacent ash-blanketed lands brought in more. And much sodium was very likely contributed by hot springs, some of which are still active in the region. So, although the trona beds accumulated as sediments in a lake, they had their ultimate origin in volcanic processes from within the earth.

Borax

Unlike trona, which is a latecomer on the commercial scene, borax has been used for centuries. Artisans in Asia Minor and the Far East used it in welding and brazing precious metals, and in glazing fine chinaware. (The word borax comes from an Arabic word, *bouraq*; the mineral is sometimes called *tincal*, a term of Malay origin.) In the thirteenth century, Marco Polo brought borax crystals to Europe. Deposits were discovered in Italy in 1771; others have been found in Chile and Turkey.

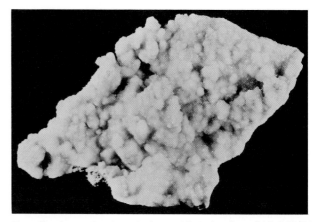

Crystalline borax. Specimen is about eight inches long. (U.S. BORAX photograph.)

In the United States, borax production began in 1864 when crystals were obtained from mineral springs and lakes north of San Francisco. Larger deposits were later found in Nevada, and in Death Valley, California, locality of the celebrated 20-mule teams. By 1887, the United States was the chief world supplier of borax, even though the country's biggest deposit was yet to be found. In 1925, drilling revealed a massive bed of borax at shallow depth at a place in the Mojave Desert now known as Boron. A large open pit today supplies more than half the world's supply of borax. Much of the remainder comes from mines in Turkey.

Borax is a clear to translucent mineral that occurs in crystals and crystalline clusters. It is a

Rich but unwanted. Kernite, a sodium borate mineral, occurs with borax and has a higher content of boric oxide. However, it is less soluble; and its fibers tend to clog the handling equipment, so it is not mined. (U.S. BORAX photograph.)

sodium borate, with an unusually large amount— 10 molecules—of water: $Na_2B_4O_7 \cdot 10H_2O$. The mineral has good fluxing qualities—that is, when combined with the raw materials of glass it lowers the temperature at which they will melt. This not only reduces the required heat energy but also makes the melt less viscous and easier to handle. Half of the U.S. consumption goes into special grades of glass, for example, heat-resistant oven-ware, and into glass fiber for insulation and textiles. A relatively new use is the flameproofing of a fluffy, low-density thermal insulation made from shredded newspaper. Borax is a raw material of boric acid and of soaps and detergents. A little borax replenishes the supply taken from the soil, but too much has a toxic effect, so the mineral is also used as a weedkiller and pesticide.

The deposit at Boron, California, accumulated in a desert lake in Pliocene time, somewhat more than 2,000,000 years ago. Borax, and a kindred mineral called kernite, occur as bedded deposits, from a few feet to more than 35 feet thick, in a gray shale. The claylike shale is impervious and has protected the borate minerals from solution in underground water. The material mined is about 75 percent borax and 25 percent shale. The borax is separated and refined in a plant adjacent to the pit and is shipped by rail.

This deposit is apparently the only one of its kind in North America. Its origin is almost certainly connected with volcanic activity. Lava flows of

Night view of processing plant at Boron, California. Borax solution is fed to crystallizing units in the tall structures. Under reduced pressure, borax drops out of solution as tiny crystals, which are allowed to grow to the desired size. (U.S. BORAX photograph.)

Pliocene age are close by; evidently boron-rich hot waters were extruded with the lava. Accumulating in the adjacent desert basin from time to time, these waters evaporated and borax was precipitated. Mud that was washed into the basin covered and protected the soluble salts. Although the whole deposit occupies less than 1 square mile, it is one of the world's major concentrations of a valuable industrial mineral.

Sulfur

Native sulfur is a bright yellow mineral with a resinous luster. It melts at 110°C (230°F), burns with a blue flame, and gives off sulfur dioxide gas (SO_2). Sulfur combines with a number of metallic elements to form a group of minerals termed sulfides. The best known of these is iron disulfide, FeS_2, which is pyrite or fool's gold. Sulfides of copper, zinc, and lead are the most important ores of those metals. Sulfur is also present in gypsum, and in hydrogen sulfide, H_2S, a gas that occurs as a minor constituent of much crude oil and natural gas.

Sulfur is so important as an industrial raw material that its consumption is one of the indexes by which a nation's technological development is measured. About 85 percent of this country's consumption is used in the form of sulfuric acid, H_2SO_4, "the king of chemicals." A large proportion of this acid is used in the manufacture of fertilizer from phosphate-bearing rock. The remainder of the sulfur and sulfuric acid is used in petroleum refining and in making chemicals, paints and pigments, iron and steel, rayon and film, industrial

Open pit at Boron, California: the free world's major source of borax. The pit is 500 feet deep; average height of benches is 60 feet. Ore goes to the plant beyond the pit, tailings to ponds at right. Mojave Desert in background, with Rogers Dry Lake in distance. (U.S. BORAX photograph.)

explosives, paper, dyes, rubber, insecticides, and a long list of other products. It is safe to say that sulfur goes into practically everything that we eat, wear, and use.

If sulfur is so widely used, why do we never see any? And why do we encounter sulfuric acid only in the laboratory of Chemistry I, where we learn that it burns holes in our skin and clothing? The answer is that sulfur and its acid are used only at intermediate stages of manufacture, somewhere between raw material and finished product. Much of the sulfur used in manufacturing is discarded as waste somewhere along the line. Any that remains in products that we see and use, like matches or automobile tires, is always combined with other materials. Even with these facts in mind, it is startling to find that every citizen of the United States "consumes" 300 pounds of sulfuric acid every year!

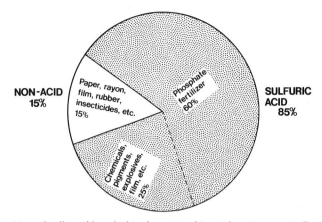

Uses of sulfur. Although this element and its acid go into practically everything we use, their production is most closely related to that of phosphate fertilizer.

Sulfur has been used for thousands of years. Primitive peoples burned it as a sort of incense to drive away evil spirits. It was also used in

Sulfur mine at the Caillou Island salt dome, Louisiana. The power plant, which heats about 2.5 million gallons of water a day, is in the distance. White-roofed building to its right is living quarters for 90 persons. Rig in foreground is drilling a sulfur well. Elevated pipeways carry hot water to sulfur wells and molten sulfur to collection station at left, thence to an insulated barge. The many small structures just above the water surface are oil wells, unrelated to sulfur production; the extension that crosses the center of the view serves these wells. (Courtesy of Freeport Sulphur Company.)

medicines and in various arts and crafts. Demand was small until about 1200 A.D., when gunpowder, which contains 10 to 15 percent sulfur, became important in warfare. Early in the seventeenth century a German alchemist, Johann Glauber, discovered how to make sulfuric acid. This shortly assumed its place as the cheapest and most versatile of the mineral acids, contributing materially to the growth of the chemical industries in the following century.

During all this time, the chief source of sulfur was the island of Sicily, where the element occurs in native form in deposits of volcanic origin. Since the Sicilians had a virtual monopoly, they tended to demand high prices. As a result, in the mid-1800s many consumers shifted to pyrite as a raw material. This is a relatively common mineral, from which sulfur may readily be obtained by a simple process of "roasting." Then, in 1895, the Frasch method of mining native sulfur came on the scene (see Chapter 3), and Texas and Louisiana rapidly became the dominant sources of supply. By 1913 the United States was the world leader in sulfur production, a position that it retains to this day.

Much natural gas contains hydrogen sulfide, a potentially corrosive substance that smells like rotten eggs and must be removed before gas can be put into the pipeline. Since the 1950s, sulfur derived from the "scrubbing" of natural gas has become increasingly important as a source of supply. Another source, which is of great significance for the future, has arisen as a result of efforts to protect the environment. Sulfurous compounds released in the smelting of sulfide ores, for example, are vented to the atmosphere in much smaller amounts than formerly—although apparently they are still one of the sources of "acid rain" in the northeastern United States and eastern Canada. In fact, sulfur is now removed from all sorts of effluents and wastes from manufacturing processes. Today, 51 percent of U.S. production is native sulfur produced by the Frasch process, but within a decade or two this proportion will probably decline by half, and 75 percent will come from sulfur-bearing natural gases, smelters, coal-burning power plants, and general manufacturing processes.

This circumstance is of more than merely statistical interest to the sulfur industry. For one thing, the new sources are widely dispersed rather than concentrated in a few native-sulfur provinces such as the Gulf Coast. For another, the sulfur is produced as a by-product or coproduct by companies that are primarily concerned with producing something else. Thus, it will be difficult to know in advance where the sulfur will be coming from or how much will be arriving on the market.

Sulfur in its different forms is produced worldwide, no one country being predominant. World production in 1978 totalled 54 million tons. The United States, in the lead, produced 21 percent; an additional 63 percent came from the U.S.S.R., Canada, Poland, Japan, France, West Germany, Mexico, mainland China, and Spain. The remaining 16 percent was distributed among 60 other countries. There is an extensive world trade in sulfur.

If, as predicted, large quantities of sulfur are to be recovered from wastes for environmental protection, a future oversupply is possible. To anticipate that situation, much research is being done on new uses. For example, it seems likely that sulfur can replace as much as 50 percent of asphalt in conventional highway paving compositions—a

Molten sulfur from a barge is deposited in a storage vat, where it will cool and solidify. (Courtesy of Freeport Sulphur Company.)

significant factor, because asphalt is in short supply and very costly. A Brazilian report suggests that molten sulfur, substituting for cement, may be mixed with sand and cast into building blocks as a means of producing low-cost housing in developing countries. The sulfur requires little energy for melting, needs no water in processing, can be used with all types of aggregate, and can be molded into precise and smooth shapes, such as interlocking blocks that require no mortar in setting up. More sophisticated uses are being investigated by companies, government agencies, and trade organizations. Whether new applications will keep pace with the projected increase in supply remains to be seen.

Fluorspar

At ordinary temperatures, the element *fluorine* is a pale yellow gas. Its name is derived from the Latin *fluere*, to flow, and alludes to its peculiar ability to flow like a liquid from a container. Since fluorine is both corrosive and poisonous, it is fortunate for all of us that it does not occur as a native element, but is always in combination with other elements. Although fluorine is present in a number of minerals—topaz, for example—it is of commercial value only in the form of calcium fluoride, CaF_2. This is the mineral *fluorite* in correct scientific usage. In commerce, it goes under the name of *fluorspar*.

Fluorite is a common mineral in vein and lode deposits, where it is often associated with quartz, barite, and metallic ores. It is transparent to translucent and ranges from colorless through shades of blue, purple, green, and yellow. Fluorite occurs as cubic crystals and crystalline aggregates and is among the most beautiful of the common minerals. The Greeks and Romans carved drinking cups and vases from exceptionally large crystals or crystalline masses.

Modern uses of fluorspar are entirely utilitarian. In steelmaking, a small proportion of the mineral aids melting, helps to transfer sulfur and phosphorus from the ore into the slag, and makes the slag fluid so that it can be readily drawn off from the molten metal. From 2 to 20 pounds of fluorspar is used for every ton of steel produced. The mineral serves a similar function in iron foundries. About 60 percent of the fluorspar consumed

is used in these and allied metallurgical applications.

A second major use of fluorspar is in the manufacture of hydrofluoric acid, HF. This is a highly reactive substance that must be handled with great care. It cannot be stored in glass containers because it dissolves glass and other silicates. About 56 pounds of hydrofluoric acid per ton of aluminum is used in refining that metal from its ore. The acid also goes into production of the organic compounds known as *fluorocarbons*. These are used in refrigerants, solvents, resins, pharmaceuticals, and a host of other products. They were formerly much used in aerosol sprays, but this use has been curtailed. There is evidence that aerosol fluorocarbons, which contain chlorine and are more accurately termed *fluoro-chloro-carbons*, may rise to the stratosphere, where, under ultraviolet radiation, they may break down and liberate free chlorine. This then may react with

"Coontail ore": fluorspar in a mine in southern Illinois. Light bands are pure fluorspar, dark bands contain fluorspar and other minerals. The beds above and below are limestone.

ozone (O_3) and reduce it to ordinary oxygen (O_2). Such weakening of the "ozone layer" in the stratosphere would allow more ultraviolet radiation to reach the earth's surface than at present, possibly increasing the incidence of skin cancer and eye damage, and conceivably even modifying the earth's climate.

Sodium fluoride, added to drinking water, raises the fluoride content to about 1 part per million. This reduces the incidence of tooth decay, particularly in children, by as much as 60 percent. Fluorides have also been added to some toothpastes.

Fluorspar lowers the temperature of fusion in making optical and other specialty glasses. Opaline and colored glasses contain 10 to 20 percent fluorspar, which makes them opaque. The mineral is also used in opaque enamels for household appliances, and for decorative brick and tile facings. There is a long list of additional uses, most of which are highly specialized.

The United States produces about 170,000 tons of fluorspar per year, mostly from underground mines in southern Illinois and western Kentucky, where the mineral occurs in veins and bedded deposits in limestone. But this is far less than enough to meet industrial needs: this country imports nearly 1,000,000 tons per year. The imported fluorspar comes chiefly from Mexico, which is the world's largest producer. Fluorspar is also produced in Italy, Spain, the Republic of South Africa, and at least 15 other countries.

Notwithstanding the wide distribution of deposits, the world's known resources of fluorspar are expected to be exhausted before the end of this century. Unless new deposits are found, the demand for fluorine will probably be met from phosphate rock, which contains about 3 percent fluorine (see Chapter 8). Resources of phosphate rock are very large, and it seems inevitable that they will eventually replace fluorspar as a source of an essential industrial element.

6.

Insulation, Mud, Diamonds . . .

The physical properties possessed by certain rocks and minerals make them of great value. The fibrous structure of asbestos and the tremendous surface area of diatomite have already been noted. Several other rocks and minerals are unusually light, heavy, fine-grained, hard, or otherwise exceptional.

Two Lightweights

Perlite. One of the products formed in certain volcanic eruptions is a viscous lava rich in silica. If cooling conditions are such that mineral crystals have no time to form, this lava congeals as a natural glass. Well-known examples are the obsidian flows in Yellowstone National Park. Obsidian was chipped into arrowheads and spear points by the Indians, but it has no commercial value today. A sister rock, however, was formed in much the same way and yields a highly valuable product. This is the rock called *perlite*.

Perlite is typically light gray and has a glassy to waxy appearance. Some perlite contains little spheres with concentric shells, like tiny onions, which were produced by internal stresses as a result of rapid cooling. These pearl-shaped spheres give the rock its name.

Most natural glasses contain water, derived from their steamy volcanic source and incorporated into the rock as it cooled. The water content of perlite is 2 to 6 percent. Now when grains of crushed perlite are abruptly heated to above 870°C (1600°F), two things happen. The grains begin to soften as their melting point is approached; and their contained water is converted into steam. As a result, each grain fluffs up, or "pops," like popcorn. A volume increase of 20

Popping perlite. One ounce of crushed perlite at left makes the expanded perlite at right. (Courtesy of Perlite Institute, Inc.)

times is not uncommon. The cooled product consists of white beads of glass foam, each bead full of tiny glass-sealed bubbles. Crude perlite weighs about 145 pounds per cubic foot, but expanded perlite can be produced that weighs as little as 2 pounds per cubic foot—truly a featherweight substance. Most of the expanded product,

Glass foam: a grain of expanded perlite, greatly enlarged. (Courtesy of Perlite Institute, Inc.)

however, has a weight in the range of 7 to 15 pounds per cubic foot.

Uses abound for this porous lightweight material. More than 60 percent is used in the construction industry as an aggregate in plaster, concrete, and wallboard. In these applications the perlite reduces the deadweight of walls, ceilings, panels, and roof decks. It is fire-resistant and sound-absorbing, and it provides good thermal insulation because of the air locked up in each tiny grain. Expanded perlite in loose bulk form is a good insulator when used to fill the spaces in hollow concrete blocks and floor and wall tile. A second major field of application is in the filtration of liquids, where expanded perlite has some of the same properties as diatomite (Chapter 4). In agriculture, the product is used as a soil conditioner for rooting seedlings and as a carrier for insecticides. There are at least a dozen minor uses.

Since crude perlite is a volcanic rock, all U.S. deposits are found in the far west where volcanism has been active in the last 15 million years or so. Perlite is mined in Arizona, California, Colorado, Idaho, and Nevada, but more than 85 percent comes from New Mexico. The largest deposit is at a site with the graphic name of No Agua (no water) in mountainous country some 70 miles north of Santa Fe and 20 miles south of the Colorado line. Three companies maintain open-pit mines in hills above a central valley. Perlite underlies the entire area; it appears to have been emplaced as a sort of volcanic upwelling or dome. It may be that the material was extruded from several vents and coalesced to form one huge mass. There are millions of tons in reserve.

Trucks haul the rock a short distance to a mill where it is crushed, dried, and screened into size grades. The screened and classified perlite is then trucked 23 miles to the railhead at Antonito, Colorado. It is shipped in crude form to plants that expand it near the point of use. Eighty plants in 33 states produce expanded perlite. The industry is young; commercial production did not start until 1946. By 1979, some 660,000 tons of perlite was produced annually in the United States. World demand outside this country, which was estimated

Perlite pit in New Mexico. Overburden has been removed, and entire hill is ready for mining. (Courtesy of Perlite Institute, Inc.)

Crude and expanded vermiculite. The commercial product is in small grains. (Courtesy of W. R. Grace & Co.)

in 1978 at more than 1 million tons, is supplied chiefly by mines in Greece, Italy, Hungary, and the U.S.S.R.

Vermiculite. In 1916, a gentleman by the name of E. N. Alley was prospecting in the mountains of northwestern Montana, near the town of Libby. He was looking for vanadium, which was in demand as a steel-hardening agent during World War I. While searching in a small tunnel, Alley observed that flakes of a coarse mica-like mineral would swell tremendously when heated by the flame of his candle. This flaky mineral proved to be *vermiculite.* Further examination showed that it was present in great quantities. Alley then forgot about vanadium. With several others, he incorporated a company to develop the vermiculite deposit. Today, the Libby mine is the largest producer of this mineral in the world.

A close relative of mica, vermiculite is a bronze, brown, or black mineral. It is a magnesium silicate with a small but crucially important content of chemically combined water. This water gives the mineral its commercial value. On exposure for a few seconds to temperatures of 800° to 1100°C (1500° to 2000°F), the water in a grain of vermiculite flashes into steam, and the particle then increases in volume by 15 to 30 times. Expansion takes place at right angles to the flat dimension of the flaky particle; it resembles the opening-out of an accordion. Thus, elongated particles are formed. Many of these are curved, and their resemblance to worms gives vermiculite its name: "little-worm stone."

Expanded vermiculite commonly has a silvery to golden hue. It weighs only 5 to 10 pounds per cubic foot—about one-twentieth the weight of the crude material—and contains so much air space that it makes an excellent heat insulator. In addition, expanded vermiculite is inert and is unaffected by high temperatures. Coarser grades provide thermal insulation in buildings and around steam pipes, pipelines carrying molten sulfur, and the like. At one time a Canadian steel company shipped red-hot steel ingots 180 miles by rail, from open hearth to mill, embedded in loose vermiculite. The temperature loss was less than 9 percent. The vermiculite was re-used.

Finer grades are used in concrete for roof decks and prefabricated panels, where light weight, thermal insulation, and sound-deadening properties

The world's largest vermiculite mine, at Libby, Montana. Rock is selectively removed in 30-foot benches and conveyed to the storage and blending dome to right of center. At the mill it is screened and dried for shipment in crude (unexpanded) form. Overburden and coarse waste are dumped in foreground; fine waste goes to settling ponds. (Courtesy of W. R. Grace & Co.)

are important. Vermiculite plasters are sprayed onto structural members as lightweight fireproofing material. Home gardeners use vermiculite for starting plant cuttings and for lightening the soil. The material absorbs moisture and odors in such household items as garbage pails and litter boxes.

The deposit at Libby, Montana, is situated on steep slopes above the valley of Rainy Creek (which is well named). As the mineral is soft and easily dug, little blasting is required; shovels load it into trucks, which take it to a nearby plant for drying and screening to size. It is then trucked to the mouth of Rainy Creek, where it is taken across the Kootenai River by overhead conveyor to loading facilities on the railroad. Since Libby is far from market centers, vermiculite is shipped in crude form and is expanded at plants near the places where it is to be used. Vermiculite has also been produced for many years from small deposits in South Carolina, and in 1978 a mine started production in northern Virginia (see Chapter 10).

Although the deposit at Libby, Montana, was in operation by 1921, output remained small until after World War II. Production in 1940 was only 22,000 tons. By 1979, it had risen to 346,000 tons, and vermiculite was being expanded at 47 plants in 30 states. Vermiculite is known to occur in many countries, but the only one comparable in importance to the United States is the Republic of South Africa. Here large deposits occur at a locality called Palabora in the Transvaal province. South African production in 1977 was estimated at 250,000 tons. Some 40,000 tons of this was imported into the eastern United States, largely because of much cheaper freight rates for ocean-borne cargoes than for overland transportation by rail.

In most of its markets, vermiculite is in strong competition with perlite. The latter has held the lead in recent years, in part because of price: in 1979, perlite sold for $104 per ton, vermiculite for $147. Vermiculite must also meet competition from imports. No doubt other factors enter the picture, such as marketing strategy, development and promotion of new uses for the product, freight rates, and simply customer preference.

How to Drill an Oil Well

Drilling wells for oil and gas is a highly specialized and technical operation, especially because many

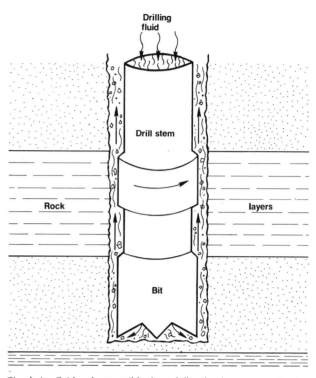

Circulating fluid makes possible deep drilling by the rotary method. It lubricates the bit and lifts the rock chips off the bottom of the hole. Bentonite and barite are common in drilling fluids.

wells are now 10,000 to 20,000 feet deep or even deeper. The actual drilling is done by a steel bit at the bottom of a length of steel pipe, the "drill string." The drill string is turned by a "rotary table" on the oil rig, and the bit bores its way downward through the rock layers. Additional lengths of drill string are added as the well gets deeper. Obviously it is necessary to continuously remove the ground-up rock from the bottom of the hole, to keep it from clogging the bit and to expose fresh rock surfaces. Furthermore, the bit must be lubricated and cooled. To meet these needs, while drilling proceeds a fluid is pumped from the surface down the inside of the drill string, through holes in the bit, and back up to the surface in the space between the drill string and the wall of the hole. It carries the rock chips to a pit on the surface, where they are removed before the fluid is recirculated.

Bentonite. In the early days of rotary drilling, water was mixed with almost any claylike soil that happened to be handy, and the drilling fluid came to be called "mud." Sometimes it is still called that, but today's drilling fluids are highly specialized compounds that must perform under extreme conditions of depth, temperature, and pressure. A mineral that plays a vital role in these fluids, and thus in the production of oil and gas, is *bentonite*.

Bentonite is a variety of clay. The type used in well drilling is unique because it absorbs large volumes of water, swelling greatly as it does so. Most of the bentonite particles are finer than one-half micron (5 ten-thousandths of a millimeter) in diameter, and, once dispersed in water, they remain in suspension indefinitely. In other words, they form a "colloidal gel" from which the solid particles will not settle out or separate. This is a highly useful property in the drilling operation. Periodically, in drilling, the bit becomes dull and must be replaced. It is then necessary to stop drilling and pull the drill string from the hole, section by section. The sections of drill string are stacked in the rig until the bit is finally recovered, removed, and replaced. Then the process has to be repeated in reverse, lowering the string back into the hole until the new bit is on the bottom and drilling can be resumed. Drillers call changing the bit "making

a round trip." It generally takes several hours. Now, while all this has been going on the mud has been sitting undisturbed in the hole. Its bentonite content keeps it from separating, and the mud retains its gelatinous character from top to bottom.

Bentonite is slippery and thus is a good lubricant for the bit. The dispersed clay not only helps lift the ground-up rock from the bottom of the hole, but it also plasters the walls of the hole, preventing unwanted water from entering and making it easy to rotate the drill string. The cost of drilling oil and gas wells is high: more than $20,000 per thousand feet for wells on land, and $70,000 or more per thousand feet for offshore wells. Since most of this cost is rental for the drilling rig, rapid drilling rates are desired. Performance of drilling fluids is important, and bentonite plays a key role.

Bentonite is named from a geologic formation called the Benton shale, which in turn was named

Bentonite in action: drilling fluid at an oil well being drilled in Nigeria. (Courtesy of Shell Photographic Service.)

from Fort Benton, Montana. Most of the bentonite used in well drilling comes from Wyoming, South Dakota, and Montana, where it occurs near the surface in flat-lying beds of Cretaceous age (about 80 million years ago). These beds can readily be mined in open pits. (In origin it is a weathered and altered volcanic ash.) The bentonite is ground to fine powder; little other milling is necessary.

Its unusual properties also make bentonite useful as a binder in holding foundry sands together to receive molten metal in casting, and as a binder in finely ground iron ore to "pelletize" the ore and make it easy to ship and handle. Some bentonite is imported, chiefly from Greece and Italy. Even though transportation charges are a large fraction of its cost, bentonite will continue to be necessary in all these uses, particularly in helping to find oil and gas.

Barite: a heavyweight. It you picked up a chunk of barite—a grayish ordinary-looking nonmetallic mineral—your first reaction would almost certainly be "Wow! It's *heavy!*" That it is. This mineral has a specific gravity of 4.2 to 4.5—well over 4 times as heavy as water and 1.7 times as heavy as granite. Barite is barium sulfate, $BaSO_4$. More than 90 percent of the barite produced is ground to powder and is used by the oil industry as an additive to drilling fluids. Thus, it may accompany bentonite. But its value rests on the property that caught your attention: its high specific gravity.

Beds of high-quality barite, marked with a white stripe, at a deposit in the Shoshone Range, Nevada. Material between the barite beds is chert (flint). (U.S. Geological Survey.)

In many of the world's oil- and gas-bearing provinces—for example, the Gulf Coast of the United States—wells are routinely drilled to depths in the range of 15,000 to 20,000 feet. At these depths, pockets of gas under very high pressure may be encountered. The drill bit may penetrate a rock with gas under so much pressure that, if uncontrolled, would blow the drill string out of the hole, wreck the rig, and quite possibly catch fire. Such disasters may be avoided by loading the drilling mud with a weighting agent, making the mud column so heavy that gas pressures are unable to lift it out of the hole. Barite is ideally suited for this purpose. It is not only heavy but also inert and clean. It mixes readily with water and bentonite. Thus, it is used worldwide for deep hazardous drilling.

Of the 10 percent of barite that is not used in well drilling, some is ground very fine and used as a filler, especially in paint. Much of the rest is converted into barium carbonate and half a dozen other barium chemicals. These go into a wide spectrum of products, from TV picture tubes and optical glass to green signal flares, fireworks, and tracer bullets.

About four-fifths of the U.S. supply of barite comes from the Battle Mountain and Toquima Range areas of central Nevada. Here dark gray barite occurs in sedimentary beds as much as 50 feet thick, interbedded with flinty rock and silica-rich shale. The material is mined in open pits. In some deposits the barite is so pure that it can simply be washed and crushed before shipment, but most of it requires upgrading by one or more of the methods described in Chapter 3. Other important deposits are found in Missouri, Arkansas, and Georgia. At a unique operation near Petersburg in southeastern Alaska, barite is drilled, blasted, and removed from a deposit beneath 60 to 120 feet of sea water.

Barite is shipped in crushed form to grinding plants near the points of use. These plants are concentrated in Texas and Louisiana, close to Gulf Coast oil fields and to tidewater port facilities. The fact that the major barite deposits in the United States are situated far from oil-rich regions means that overland transportation costs are high. To deliver a ton of barite to the Gulf Coast by rail from Nevada costs more than to send a ton by ocean freighter from Ireland. Although the United States produces 1.5 million tons of barite per year, it imports an additional million tons, chiefly from Ireland, Peru, and Mexico. Domestic demand is expected to grow until about 1990, after which it will presumably decline as the country's drilling tapers off.

Kaolin: From Clay Pit to Coffee Table

The mineral *kaolin* takes its name from the Chinese "kauling," meaning high hill and referring to a locality where this unusual white clay was found. The term *china clay* is sometimes still applied to kaolin, especially in England, where it has been mined and used since the early 1700s, notably by Josiah Wedgwood in his famous chinaware. Though kaolin is still used in whiteware, wall tile, and the like, a newer use far overshadows the older one. This use is in the production of high-quality paper.

Paper? Everybody knows that paper is made from wood pulp. Wood is ground up, and the pulp is chemically treated so that it can be formed into a thin sheet of intermeshed and felted fibers—like ordinary newsprint. But such paper, though cheap and adequate for its purpose, is neither strong nor durable. Furthermore, it is not very white, nor is it smooth enough to reproduce sharp photographic images. A much higher grade of paper is required for a picture magazine, a company's annual report, or a beautifully illustrated book that might find its way onto your coffee table. Paper for this type of product contains, in addition to wood pulp, up to 30 percent of kaolin.

A far cry from ordinary clay, kaolin has an array of properties that make it ideally suited for use in paper. It is brilliant white, extremely fine-grained, soft, free from grit, chemically inert, and easily dispersed in water. It is also opaque, having what is called "good covering power." It produces a high gloss on paper and a surface that holds ink evenly. Finally, it is relatively cheap.

In the making of high-quality paper, kaolin is introduced in a water suspension. The particles become mechanically trapped among the wood fibers. This gives the paper a closely textured surface that is brilliant white, opaque, and smooth. When the paper is polished by passage between smooth rollers—a process known as "calendering"—

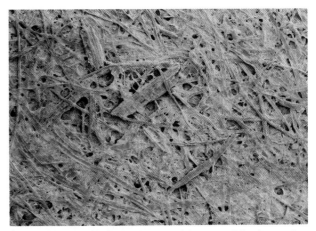

Paper, magnified 48 times, before application of kaolin coating. (Courtesy of Yara Engineering Corporation.)

it becomes usable for a wide variety of printing applications. But even such "filled paper" is not smooth enough for reproducing illustrations of the finest quality. For this purpose the paper's surface is coated with a thin film of extra-fine kaolin suspended in an adhesive mixture. This coating buries the fibers and prevents them from absorbing the ink. After calendering, a coated paper will accept ink uniformly and reproduce graphic images, either in color or in black and white, with extreme fidelity.

Kaolin is formed by the long-continued decay of the mineral feldspar, especially in such rocks as granite. Some of the world's largest deposits occur in Cornwall, southwestern England, where rocks that were once hard, fresh granite are now a soft crumbly mass of kaolin and quartz grains. High-pressure water jets, like fire hoses, are used to wash the white kaolin into pools at the bottom of

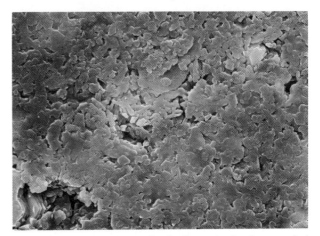

Paper, magnified 5,400 times, after kaolin coating has been applied. (Courtesy of Yara Engineering Corporation.)

A kaolin pit in Cornwall, England. The white clay is washed from the rock by a hydraulic jet (near center, just below wheeled vehicle). It flows to a sump pit from where it is pumped to the plant. Hills in background are waste sand from more than a century of mining. (Courtesy of English China Clays Group.)

Settling tanks: the first stage in refining English kaolin. In the distance are waste dumps from open-pit mines. (Courtesy of English China Clays Group.)

deep pits. Here it is separated from the quartz, which is conveyed to waste piles. The kaolin is pumped up to a plant on the surface, where it is washed, filtered, and dried.

The chief U.S. deposits, by contrast, are in flat-lying sedimentary beds, situated in Georgia and South Carolina. Streams long ago washed the kaolin from its parent rock—probably a decomposed granite—and brought it to shallow lagoons on the coastal plain. The beds of white kaolin are close to the surface and are readily dug by power shovels. The deposits are exceptionally pure, and indeed they qualify for the group of "pure rocks" discussed in Chapter 4.

In 1978, Cornwall produced 3,800,000 tons of kaolin and the Georgia-South Carolina district 6,200,000 tons; these made up 60 percent of the world's output. Nearly one million tons of the Georgia kaolin is exported, especially to Canada

Hydraulic jet washing kaolin from the decayed granitic rock in which it occurs. (Courtesy of English China Clays Group.)

Refined kaolin before filtering and drying. (Courtesy of English China Clays Group.)

and Japan, and much of the Cornwall production goes to continental Europe. Other large producing countries are Czechoslovakia, the U.S.S.R., West Germany, and India.

Since kaolin is used at the paper mill in a water dispersion, it is wasteful to filter and dry it at the point of production, package it for shipping, and then re-disperse it in water at the point of use. Consequently, much kaolin is now shipped in slurry form, for example, in tank cars from Georgia to paper mills in the upper midwest, or in specially designed vessels from Cornwall to Rotterdam or Hamburg.

Refined and dried Kaolin awaiting shipment. (Courtesy of English China Clays Group.)

The world's demand for paper—and hence for kaolin—seems insatiable. Production of kaolin increased 27 percent from 1970 to 1978 and continues to rise. And the papermakers' requirements become more stringent all the time, especially for whiteness and covering power. Lighter weight is also desired, largely because of sharply increased postal rates for books and magazines.

Flotation and magnetic separation are used to remove the last vestiges of iron-bearing minerals; bleaching with chemicals eliminates iron stain. The process of "delamination" produces an ultra-white product that commands a premium price. Each kaolin particle has a laminated structure like mica (a close relative). Attrition grinding in a specially designed tank, using plastic beads as a grinding medium, breaks down the particles into their individual platelets. These are whiter than a natural clay of similar fineness, and provide excellent coverage in paper coating at light weight. The kaolin industry devotes an exceptional amount of time and effort to research on improving the product, in order that clay may continue to make up a sizable portion of our printed matter.

Large crystals of kaolinite (the mineral of kaolin) in stacklike form. These crystals are "delaminated" into separate platelike particles for use in coating paper. Magnified 4,100 times. (Courtesy of Yara Engineering Corporation.)

Two Forms of Carbon

Carbon, though not very plentiful in the earth's crust, is a highly important element. Combined with hydrogen and oxygen, it is present in all plants and animals; it is the second most abundant element (after oxygen) in the human body. Combined with hydrogen, it forms the hydrocarbons of which coal, oil, and gas are made. Combined with oxygen, it occurs in the atmosphere as carbon dioxide, and in carbonate minerals such as calcite. Carbon also occurs alone, as two radically different minerals—graphite and diamond.

Graphite is black; gem diamond is clear and colorless, and industrial diamond (with which we are concerned) is yellow-brown to dark. Graphite is soft; diamond is the hardest natural substance known. Graphite is stable at temperatures well above 3000°C (5400°F); diamond burns up at 870°C (1600°F). Graphite has a specific gravity of 2.2; industrial diamond, 2.9 to 3.3. Graphite occurs as scales, flakes, bladed masses, and earthy lumps; diamond as small crystals or crystalline aggregates. Graphite is opaque in even the finest particles; diamond has exceptional light-gathering power, color dispersion, and play of color.

How can two minerals with identical composition be so different? The answer lies in their atomic structure. In graphite, this structure is sheetlike, with strong bonds within sheets but weak bonds between them. Thus, the mineral is soft, as adjacent sheets may readily slide over each other. In the crystal lattice of diamond, on the other hand, each carbon atom is tightly bound to four others, forming a very strong interlocked structure that extends in three dimensions. These two forms of carbon have quite different geologic histories. Most graphite is a metamorphic mineral, and shares the laminated structure of mica and other minerals of like origin; diamond is an igneous mineral, formed deep in the crust and brought near the surface by intrusion from far below.

Graphite. Because it is immune to very high temperatures, graphite is used wherever molten metal is handled. It is a prime constituent of the crucibles in which steel, aluminum, brass, and precious metals are melted. Mixed with sand or clay, it lines the molds into which the melt is poured, giving the surface of the molds a smooth finish so that castings can be easily removed after cooling. Together with another heat-resistant material, magnesium oxide, graphite makes bricks for lining the furnaces in which steel is produced. These metallurgical uses account for about two-thirds of the graphite used in the United States.

The softness and layered structure of graphite make it highly slippery or unctuous. It adheres

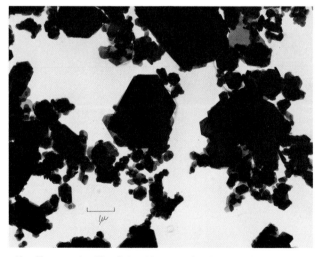

Platelike crystals of kaolinite. After size classification, they are used in paper coating. Magnified 21,000 times; the line is one micron (one-thousandth of a millimeter) in length. Thicker crystals appear black because they are opaque to the electron beam; thinner ones are translucent. (Courtesy of Yara Engineering Corporation.)

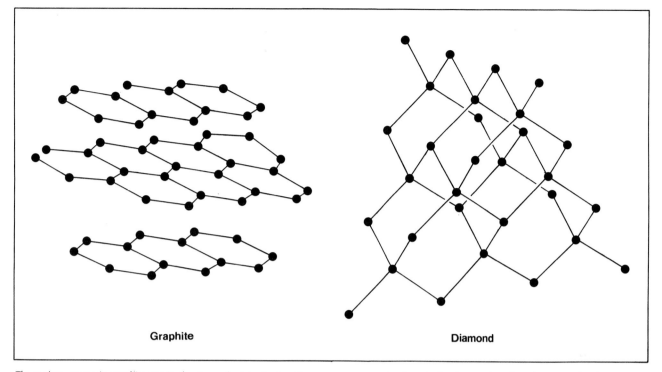

Graphite

Diamond

The carbon atoms in graphite are in sheets, each atom having three nearest neighbors; the sheets are weakly bonded and can readily slide over each other. In the diamond, each carbon atom has four nearest neighbors, giving a rigid interlocked structure in three dimensions.

readily to metal, filling the pores and making a slick surface. As a result, it is widely used as a lubricant, especially in applications where oil or grease might be harmful, as in textile machinery, or where high temperatures are encountered, as in rolling mills for steel. About 5 percent of the country's consumption is for this use. Graphite is an excellent conductor of electricity and so is used in carbon brushes for electric motors. Among the many other products in which the mineral is important are dry-cell batteries; "lead" pencils; and protective paint for bridges, tanks, and similar structures. (So-called "graphite fibers," used in such items as fishing rods and tennis rackets, are extremely strong and elastic. But they are not really graphite; they are carbon filaments manufactured from rayon or other fibrous carbon-bearing raw material.)

Graphite is one of the few nonmetallic minerals that is not produced in the United States. High-quality flake graphite for use in crucibles is imported from the Malagasy Republic (the island of Madagascar); pure massive or "lump" graphite comes from Sri Lanka (Ceylon). Large deposits have been mined since 1895 in the state of Sonora,

western Mexico. Other producing countries include East Germany, Austria, Czechoslovakia, India, and North Korea. The mineral varies in purity and physical properties among these deposits. Many consumers have developed formulas and requirements based on graphite from a specific group of deposits, or even from a certain mine, and are reluctant to change to other sources. This gives international trade in graphite certain constraints that are absent from most commerce in earth materials.

World production of graphite in 1979 was about 500,000 tons; of this, the United States consumed about 60,000 tons. Most of the remainder went to western Europe and Japan. The flourishing Japanese steel industry has made Japan an increasingly important consumer of graphite.

Diamond. The gem diamond is still the most desired of precious stones, as it has been for centuries. In recent decades, however, the diamond has come to occupy an essential place in industry, and today about 90 percent of world production of the natural stone is of industrial grade. Industrial diamond consists of material that is off-color, flawed, or broken and hence is unsuited for use as gems. Synthetic diamond, which has been manufactured since the 1950s, now accounts for more than half of the total produced. It is made by subjecting graphite to very high temperatures and pressures in the presence of a metal catalyst. Synthetic diamond is mostly in the form of fine grit.

By virtue of its hardness, the diamond stands alone as an abrasive. It is especially well adapted to automated cutting and grinding processes, which are left unattended for long periods. Diamond dust is used for polishing gem diamonds, etching glass, and the like. Diamond grit finds its most important use in saw blades and grinding wheels. The diamond wheel is the means by which such hard tools as tungsten-carbide bits (used by miners in rock drilling) are sharpened, milled, and ground to close tolerances.

Cores of rock below the surface can be obtained by drilling with a ring-shaped bit set with diamond chips. The diamond core drill is a major exploration tool for all sorts of mining exploration, as well as in evaluation of dam sites, tunnels, and deep foundations. Large diamonds are used in wire-drawing dies. A sound diamond crystal of good quality is drilled from opposite sides by a needle moistened with olive oil impregnated with diamond dust. The hole on one side is funnel-shaped, on the other bell-shaped. If the two holes are exactly centered, a final breakthrough no larger than 0.0003 inch (three ten-thousandths of an inch) may be made. Fine wire for lamps and precision instruments is drawn through a series of dies, each smaller than the last, and filaments may be produced with a fraction of the diameter of a human hair. Diamond dies have a very slow rate of wear and will retain their original dimension for a long time.

The primary source of diamond is a dark green igneous rock called *kimberlite*. This rock apparently originates deep within the crust, or even in the underlying mantle, and has been intruded or thrust upward through the overlying rocks in vertical columns known as "pipes." The best-known and most productive pipes are in the Kimberley district of South Africa, where they have long been mined, both in deep open pits and underground. But only a small part of today's production of industrial stones comes from kimberlite. Many diamond-bearing regions, including those of South Africa, have been deeply eroded by streams. As a

Moving the earth for diamonds. These big machines remove beach sand to get at underlying diamond-bearing gravel. Shoreline of Namibia (South West Africa); Atlantic Ocean at top of view. (Courtesy of Peter Silveri Associates, Inc.)

result, diamond and other resistant minerals are to be found in deposits of stream gravel, or, if carried to the sea, in recent or elevated marine beaches. Many of these alluvial deposits are far from any known occurrence of kimberlite. Even in deposits that are said to be "rich," the diamond is scarcely an abundant mineral: to obtain 1 gram, it is necessary to remove and process 25 tons of rock!

Diamond is recovered from alluvial gravels and sands by washing, screening, and other relatively simple mechanical processes. The object is to separate the light minerals, such as quartz and clay, from the heavier fraction, and then to separate the diamond from the other heavy minerals. At Kimberley in 1896, a heavy-mineral concentrate accidentally came into contact with some axle grease. To everyone's surprise, the diamonds stuck to the grease, whereas the associated minerals did not. A grease-coated table or a grease belt shortly became a standard part of the processing circuit. The concentrate is washed across such a surface as a regular part of the milling process.

Though the United States is the largest consumer of industrial diamond, it has no commercial resources of the natural mineral. The world's largest producer is the Republic of Zaire in central

Africa; the U.S.S.R. ranks second and the Republic of South Africa third. Other producing countries are Namibia (South West Africa), Angola, and Ghana. Only minor production comes from the western hemisphere, in Venezuela and Brazil. In the late 1970s, exploration for kimberlite pipes and alluvial deposits got under way in western Australia, and this country may shortly be added to the list of producers. Synthetic diamond is manufactured in the United States, the Republic of South Africa, Ireland, Sweden, the U.S.S.R., and Japan.

The standard unit of weight in the diamond is the metric carat, or one-fifth gram. World production of natural diamond in 1977 totalled 31,100,000 carats. This seems impressive, but it equals only 13,712 pounds, or less than 7 tons. Prices in the same year ranged from $4.00 per carat for small sizes to as much as $65.00 per carat for first-quality stones large enough for use in dies. This translates into $9,000 to $147,000 *per pound*.

So we are talking about a small-bulk but very high-value commodity—at the opposite end of the spectrum from crushed stone, for example, which is produced in the millions of tons but is priced at only $3 or $4 per ton. World production of synthetic diamond in 1977 was about 71,000,000 carats. Since this material was in the very fine size range, prices were much lower—just over $2.00 per carat. Because of competition and increased efficiency of production, prices of the synthetic material have been decreasing in the past 20 years. In all probability, synthetic diamonds will be produced in larger grain sizes in the future and will take over a bigger share of the market.

Diamond saw cutting structural concrete. The blade is set with small synthetic diamonds. Repeated cuts enable engineers to study the concrete unit throughout its length. (Courtesy of General Electric Company.)

7.

Minerals in Glass, Refractories, Paint

Glass and its Raw Materials

Unless you are blessed with unusually good eyesight, you are reading these words through glass. The light by which you read also comes through glass from a window or an electric fixture. Plate glass "brings the outside indoors," glass fiber insulates our buildings, and glass containers bring us much of our food and drink. In this section we take a look at a most remarkable material.

What is glass? Glass is accurately defined as a supercooled liquid—a solid liquid, if you please. To understand this seeming contradiction, we may consider the behavior of a "normal" inorganic substance, such as a metal, with respect to temperature. At a very high temperature the material is a molten liquid. As it cools, the liquid flows less and less easily—that is, its viscosity increases. At a certain temperature—the freezing point—the randomly arranged molecules in the liquid abruptly move into ordered crystalline patterns, and the material becomes a rigid solid composed of interlocking crystals. But glass doesn't behave like this. As molten glass cools, its viscosity increases so fast that the rearrangement of molecules into crystals is prevented. Thus, the glass retains the random internal structure of liquid, but in a molecular network that is immobile. On its way toward crystallinity, glass is a case of arrested development.

From this it is clear why glass is so fragile. It contains no crystal boundaries to halt the spread of a fracture, so when a crack starts it moves rapidly indeed. Furthermore, ordinary glass is a poor conductor of heat, so that any sudden temperature change at the surface is transmitted very slowly to the interior. This sets up internal stresses that may result in fracture. Only in certain special-purpose glasses is this sensitivity to temperature change overcome.

Light passes through glass without hindrance, except at the surface, from which some is reflected. Since light travels more slowly in glass than in air, glass has the ability to "bend" light rays. This is the property utilized in eyeglasses, cameras, microscopes, and other optical instruments. All of these contain lenses, which bend light to focus it in different ways.

The ingredients of glass. It is theoretically possible to produce glass from quite a number of substances, but there is just one commercial primary glass-forming compound: silica, SiO_2. Pure silica glass cannot be produced on a large scale, however, because of the extremely high temperature required—1700°C (3100°F)—and also because the glass is viscous and difficult to work. To bring the temperature of melting down to more reasonable levels, improve workability, and add certain desired properties, two bulk additions are made. These are soda ash (sodium carbonate) and limestone (calcium carbonate). These substances reduce the number of bonds in the glass network, "opening up" the network and lowering the viscosity. They allow working the glass at temperatures as low as 600°C (1100°F). In the resulting glass, the elements sodium and calcium are present as the oxides soda (Na_2O) and lime (CaO); hence the name *soda-lime-silica glass*, which applies to more than 90 percent of all the glass melted. The most common proportion of these compounds in glass is about 70 percent

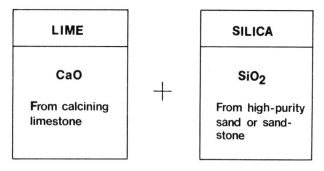

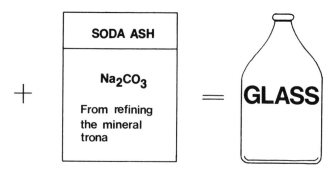

Ingredients of glass. Additional compounds are introduced to make heat-resistant glass and other special types.

silica, 15 percent soda, and 5 to 10 percent lime. The balance is made up of alumina, magnesia, and other compounds to increase the strength or chemical resistance of the glass. Other substances may be added to counteract the effects of impurities in the raw materials, or to impart special properties such as color or opacity.

When a metallic ore is smelted, impurities in the raw materials are removed in the slag, but there is no "slagging stage" in glassmaking. Each raw material leaves a compound in the finished product: whatever goes in, stays in. Therefore, the purity of the raw materials is of the greatest importance. Silica for ordinary flat glass and containers must be at least 95 percent pure; for optical glass, over 99 percent. Iron and chromium are probably the two most troublesome impurities. Iron oxide gives a green color to glass; iron-chromium oxide is insoluble in the melt and may remain as black particles in the product. For the bulk production of glass, the consistency of the impurity content is more important than its actual value. As long as the glassmaker knows how much iron oxide, for example, is going into his product, he can modify the process accordingly; what he fears most is a sudden increase in an impurity. To make uniform glass requires ingredients of dependable uniformity.

Other raw materials. Optical glass, and the "crystal" of fine tableware, is *lead-alkali-silica* glass. It consists primarily of silica, lead oxide, and soda or potash ("alkali"). It seems strange that the element lead—which we know as a dull, heavy metal—imparts clarity and brilliance to glass, but it does. The content of lead oxide ranges from 20 percent to as high as 80 percent.

Ovenware glass, such as Pyrex, owes its heat-resistant qualities to a content of boron. Such *borosilicate* glass consists of 60 to 80 percent silica and 10 to 25 percent boric oxide, with small amounts of alumina and soda. Exceptional resistance to chemicals is provided by *aluminosilicate* glass, which is a combination of silica, alumina, and lime. It is used for laboratory glassware, industrial piping, and the like.

Coloring agents in glass include sulfur and iron sulfide (amber), the element selenium (pink), cobalt oxide (blue), and iron oxides (green, yellow, brown). Glass is rendered opaque by fluorspar, zinc oxide, or a fluoride of sodium and aluminum.

Making plate glass by the float process. Raw materials enter at left; "cullet" is recycled broken glass.

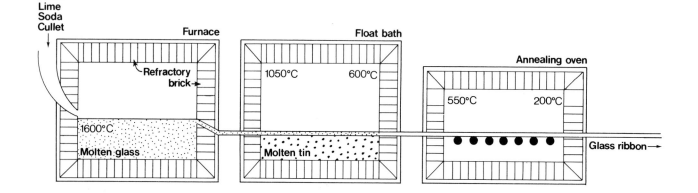

A ribbon of "float" glass, cooling to room temperature after emerging from the annealing oven in the distance. Supporting rollers show clearly, and ceiling lights are reflected without distortion. (Courtesy of PPG Industries, Inc.)

The making of glass. Four basic stages are involved in glass manufacture. In *melting*, the raw materials are thoroughly mixed, combined with waste glass, known as *cullet*, and raised to the melting range of 600–900 °C (1100–1650 °F). In the *refining* stage, the temperature is increased to about 1500 °C (2730 °F) in order to remove bubbles of carbon dioxide and other gases and to complete the reactions. The temperature is then reduced to about 1000 °C (1830 °F) for the *working* stage, in which glass is formed into the desired shape. The fourth and final stage is *annealing*. This involves re-heating the glass in order to relieve internal stresses developed during the working stage, and then slowly cooling it to room temperature.

Glass is blown, pressed, drawn, or rolled into the desired products, mostly by automated machines and mostly for flat glass and containers. A variety of specialized and sophisticated processes is involved. We cite one of these as being of special interest.

Sandstone suitable for making ordinary container glass. The rock contains a little iron oxide, most of which is removed in processing.

A vase of lead crystal glass: "Temple Jar," from a series designed by Donald Pollard. (Courtesy of Steuben Glass.)

This is the float-glass process for the production of plate glass for use in items ranging from mirrors to show windows and the walls of office buildings. From the furnace—which has a melting area 165 feet long, 30 feet wide, and 4 feet deep and holds more than 1,200 tons of molten glass—a continuous glass ribbon 13 feet wide flows onto the perfectly flat surface of a bath of molten tin. In this forming chamber, more than 150 feet long, irregularities in the glass melt down, and the upper and lower surfaces of the sheet become absolutely parallel. Before leaving the chamber, the glass is cooled enough so that it can pass onto rollers without being marked in any way. The sheet then passes through an annealing oven, from which it emerges and eventually cools to room temperature. Glass produced in this way is clear, uniform, and free of distortion. It requires no processing and is ready to be cut into sheets for use. Thicknesses ranging from one-eighth inch to as much as 1 inch can be produced. Metallic ions can be introduced to make "one-way glass" that reflects heat and glare. A typical plant produces 450 tons of glass per day.

Most glass plants are situated near sources of raw materials, especially silica sand. Availability of fuel is also of great importance, as these plants operate continuously, 24 hours a day, every day of the year, for several years until they are shut down for inspection and repair. Production of glass is definitely not a 9-to-5 operation.

Taking the Heat: Refractories

Glass, ceramics, cement, and lime, together with steel, copper, and the other metals, all have one thing in common: a stage of manufacture that involves very high temperatures. None of these products can be made without the help of heat-resistant materials, or *refractories*. Practically all the refractories used in industry are nonmetallic earth substances.

Refractory bricks. Blast furnaces, cement kilns, glassmaking tanks, and similar units are generally lined with brickwork. Although some special shapes are required, most bricks do not differ greatly in size from those used in the sides and back of an ordinary fireplace. (These bricks are different from the ones on the outside of the

Lining a cement kiln with refractory bricks. They must withstand temperatures of 1370°C (2500°F). (Courtesy of Maury Drenkel, Inc.)

fireplace. The latter would not withstand the heat in the burning area.) But there is a wide range in composition. Not only must refractory brick be able to withstand temperatures in the range of 1400 to 1800°C (2600 to 3300°F), but they must also resist impact, wear, chemical attack, and sudden changes of temperature. Not surprisingly, there is a considerable variety of these products.

The oldest type of refractory is probably brick made from *fire clay*. Important deposits of fire clay are found in the central and eastern United States, in flat-lying beds of Pennsylvanian age (300 million years ago). The typical fire clay in this region is 3 to 10 feet thick and lies immediately beneath a coal seam. The clays are composed chiefly of silica and alumina, both of which are highly resistant to heat. A plastic mixture of moist clay is pressed or extruded into brick form, and then the bricks are dried and heated, or "fired," in a kiln. The firing process drives off moisture; oxidizes iron, sulfur, and organic impurities; and heats the clay body until melting just begins. This gives the brick a dense, fused structure. Fire-clay brick is used in blast furnaces for melting iron ore, in ladles for transferring molten metal between furnaces and molds, and in ceramic kilns, glass tanks, and fireplaces.

A gray, brown, or yellowish earthy rock called *bauxite* is the chief raw material of *high-alumina brick*. Bauxite is made up of oxides of aluminum and indeed is the chief ore of that metal. It is the product of long-continued weathering of granitic rocks in warm regions of much rainfall; the major deposits are in northern South America, especially Guyana, and on the island of Jamaica. There are also deposits in Alabama. High-alumina bricks are processed in much the same way as fire-clay bricks. They will withstand higher temperatures, and are especially used in lining the rotary kilns in which cement and lime are produced and in electric furnaces for melting steel and aluminum.

A few sandstones consist almost entirely of quartz grains cemented together by quartz. Aside from a few scattered grains of other minerals and a trace of clay, such rocks are essentially pure silica. They are known as *quartzite* to geologists and as *ganister* to makers of refractories. Ganister is the raw material of *silica brick*. It is crushed, washed to remove clay, screened, and proportioned as to grain size. After addition of a clay binder, bricks are formed, dried, and fired at about 1480°C (2700°F). Because silica undergoes changes in molecular structure with rising temperature, the bricks that come out of the kiln are about 14 percent larger

than when they went in, and show a corresponding decrease in density. Silica brick is used mainly in ceramic kilns, in tanks for holding molten glass, in coke ovens, and in blast-furnace stoves. (Coke is a porous high-carbon fuel, used in steelmaking, that is produced by roasting bituminous coal in an oven. A blast-furnace stove provides preheated air to the furnace in which iron ore is melted.)

Furnaces for steelmaking are commonly lined with *basic brick*. The main constituent of basic brick is magnesia, MgO, or lime-magnesia, CaO·MgO. The parent material of magnesia is the mineral magnesite (magnesium carbonate, $MgCO_3$), which is mined in Nevada and Quebec and is also imported from Greece and Yugoslavia. Magnesite is calcined, driving off carbon dioxide and leaving MgO, which is white, dense, and highly refractory. Lime-magnesia is made in like manner from dolomite, the calcium-magnesium

Placing fire-clay mix in a form. After firing, the forms will be door shapes for coke ovens. (Courtesy of General Refractories Company.)

carbonate, CaMg(CO$_3$)$_2$. Magnesia is also produced chemically from sea water. Basic brick may be made with a content of chromite, a dark refractory mineral that comes chiefly from the Republic of South Africa. The raw materials for basic brick are crushed, ground, screened, and proportioned. Bonding may be provided by fire clay or by asphaltic material that burns away when the bricks are fired, leaving an inert bond of carbon. Firing takes place at about 1760°C (3200°F). Basic brick is used in the production of copper and nickel, as well as steel, and also lines the hottest parts of cement kilns.

Refractories that insulate. It might seem that if materials can withstand intense heat and wear, they should scarcely be asked to do more. But high temperatures mean great expenditures of costly energy. To help conserve energy, refractories have been developed that not only withstand heat but help to retain it. In preparing insulating brick from any of the raw materials we have mentioned, holes or bubbles are formed in the mix before the bricks are fired. The mix may be mechanically beaten, using a frothing agent; gas bubbles may be formed by a chemical reaction; or combustible material, such as sawdust, may be incorporated, only to burn away, leaving voids when the brick is fired. An alternate method is to introduce lightweight aggregates into the mix, such as diatomite, expanded perlite, or vermiculite. The aim is to produce enough voids in the brick to give low heat conduction, at the same time retaining adequate strength.

Some insulating refractories are in the form of ceramic fibers, such as glass fibers or "rock wool," made by blowing molten rock into threads. A

Molten steel being poured from 35-ton ladle into sand molds to make parts for railroad freight-car trucks. Metal enters the dish-shaped openings ("sprues") on right, and hot gases escape from vents at center and left. Compacted molding sand is visible on top of the molds. (Courtesy of Buckeye Steel Castings Company.)

blanket of such material over a furnace can cut heat loss dramatically.

Insulating bricks may be so efficient that they cause problems. If used behind the normal refractory linings of furnace or kiln, they may reduce heat flow so much that the lining bricks overheat and have a shorter service life than normal. Still, the cost of fuel continues to increase, and there is no doubt that further efforts will be made to produce refractories that insulate.

Molding sands. Many everyday metal objects, from water faucets to automobile engine blocks, are formed by pouring molten metal into a mold, allowing the metal to cool and harden, and breaking the mold away. Most molds include internal projections, termed cores, around which the metal flows so as to produce a hollow space in the resulting casting. The standard material for molds is a mixture of sand and clay. A few sand-clay mixtures occur in nature in just the right proportions, and these naturally bonded molding sands may be used for small castings. But today most molds are made of synthetic mixtures, in which the sand and clay are specially chosen and their proportions closely controlled.

The standard material is clean quartz sand, with a silica content of more than 95 percent and a melting point of at least 1650°C (3000°F). A moderate range in grain size—the small grains filling spaces between the larger ones—keeps the metal from penetrating into the mold and also aids resistance to thermal shock. Sand from the St. Peter sandstone, described in Chapter 4, is the standard, but several other sources of high-silica sand are also used.

Although silica sand makes up more than 90 percent of the total used in molding, three other minerals are of some importance. *Zircon,* $ZrSiO_4$, has a fusing temperature several hundred degrees above that of quartz. In making steel castings, a sand of about 65 percent zircon and 35 percent quartz may be used on the internal face of the mold, with quartz sand used as backing. The main source of zircon is Australian beach sands. *Chromite,* $FeCr_2O_4$, also has excellent refractory properties. Like zircon, it is imported. The main source of supply is the Republic of South Africa, where chromite occurs in hard rock deposits that must be mined and crushed. A third mineral that may be used is *olivine,* a magnesium-iron silicate. Like chromite, it occurs as a rock and must be processed to sand-size grains. It is less stable than zircon and chromite under thermal shock, but replaces silica sand in some foundries. The United States has olivine deposits in the states of Washington and North Carolina. At the end of 1980, zircon, chromite, and olivine of foundry grade were all priced at $70 to $75 per ton, whereas the quoted price of silica sand was about $20 per ton. Thus, economic factors clearly favor continued use of the traditional material.

From 5 to 10 percent of molding sand consists of a clay binder. The premium material for this purpose is Wyoming bentonite, of the same kind that we discussed under well drilling. The material is plastic, holds moisture well, and is thermally stable. It binds the sand in molds for steel and heavy iron castings. Some iron foundries use another variety of bentonite, which comes from bedded deposits in the coastal plain of Texas, Mississippi, and Alabama. The two types of bentonite may be blended to achieve special properties. Chemical or organic binders, such as resin, are increasing in use but do not seem to threaten the supremacy of bentonite. In foundries worldwide, some 3 million tons of bentonite is used each year, and this demand is expected to continue.

In preparing to make large castings, foundrymen often coat the inside of the mold with refractory paint. A finely ground refractory material in water or a solvent is sprayed or painted onto the surface and dried. This gives an improved finish to the casting and also makes it easy to remove the mold. Graphite, zircon, chromite, and olivine are among the materials used in such coatings.

Minerals in Paint

One-third of the contents of a can of paint consists of mineral products. Diverse and specialized, these materials merit our attention.

The nature of paint. Paint consists of three essential components. The *binder,* or "vehicle," forms a hard film on drying which adheres to the surface and gives a gloss. The volatile fraction, or *solvent,* lowers the viscosity of the binder and makes for ease of application. It evaporates after the paint is applied. The *pigment* gives the paint its color, as well as its ability to hide previous coats. This is the component with which we are concerned.

The pigment consists of very fine inert particles of either a mineral or a mineral-derived product. Fully as important as its color is its *opacity*, or hiding power. This depends in part on particle size; the smaller the particles, the greater their total surface area, reflecting ability, and hence, opacity. The ability of the powdered pigment to bend light rays—its refractive index—is also important. Finally, the solid particles must not cluster together but must remain separated in the paint system. Ease of dispersion is therefore necessary.

In addition to binder, solvent, and pigment, there is a group of materials called *additives*. These include thickeners, stabilizers, and other materials that do not need to concern us, but they also include *extenders*. These are inexpensive materials that were introduced to "extend" costly pigments—to make them go further—in order to lower costs. Because their original purpose was to dilute the pigment, they were sometimes looked on with raised eyebrows. Extenders have now been developed, however, that impart several valuable properties to paint, such as increased hiding power, gloss, brushability, and chemical resistance.

Pigments constitute about 18 percent of the raw materials used in paint manufacture, and additives about 15 percent.

The whitest of the white. Overwhelmingly the dominant paint pigment is titanium dioxide. It accounts for at least 75 percent of all pigment used. This material has a high refractive index and a hiding power several orders higher than the nearest competitor. It is manufactured from rutile (natural TiO_2) or ilmenite ($FeTiO_3$); the former is preferred, but ilmenite is more abundant and thus more generally used. Rutile is reddish brown, and ilmenite is black; it is astonishing that their derivative is brilliant white. Both minerals are found in beach sands, mainly in western Australia and in South Africa, as discussed in Chapter 3. Ilmenite is also mined from hard-rock deposits in the Adirondack Mountains of New York, and in Quebec, Norway, and Finland. Since World War II, plants for the manufacture of TiO_2 have been built in most of the industrialized countries. World production now totals more than two million tons per year.

Up to about 1945, white pigment was mainly "white lead" (lead carbonate) and other lead-based compounds. Their eclipse by TiO_2 has resulted from three factors. First, TiO_2 is better. Second, the price of lead-based pigments is controlled by that of metallic lead, and this price has been volatile and unpredictable. Third, lead has been shown to be harmful to health, and paints containing more than a tiny fraction of lead have been outlawed in the United States and other countries. Thus, "lead-free" paints have acquired a strong selling advan-

The chief mineral ingredients of paint.

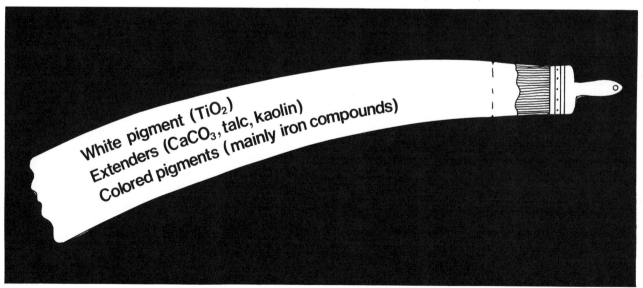

White pigment (TiO_2)
Extenders ($CaCO_3$, talc, kaolin)
Colored pigments (mainly iron compounds)

tage. The ban on lead has also affected some colored pigments, for example, certain red ones based on "red lead" (lead oxide).

The colorful compounds of iron. Red, brown, and yellow pigments are largely based on iron oxide. Natural iron oxides were the first coloring materials known to man. Cave paintings thousands of years old testify to the coloring power and stability of these pigments. The familiar red "barn paint" is a more modern example. Red colors have traditionally been derived from hematite (Fe_2O_3), yellows and yellow-browns from limonite (hydrous Fe_2O_3), and deeper browns from limonite with an admixture of manganese dioxide (MnO_2). These oxides are among the most widely distributed minerals in the earth's crust, but deposits of commercial size are rare. Hematite, known in the trade as "red ocher," is produced in Spain and Austria; it is a by-product of iron-ore mining in Michigan and is also produced from deep red clays in Georgia. Limonite, or "yellow ocher" and "sienna," is essentially clay that contains a significant content of hydrous iron oxide. Production comes from Spain, South Africa, and France. The iron-manganese oxides, or "umber," produce a rich chestnut-brown color when calcined. The sole commercial source is the island of Cyprus, where the material occurs as an earthy deposit believed to have formed on an ancient sea floor by chemical alteration of iron- and manganese-rich lavas that were erupted directly into the sea.

Green pigments are based mainly on lead-chromium oxide and various iron compounds; blue and purple, on iron compounds; and black, on magnetite or graphite. Colored pigments are marketed in highly concentrated form. They are added in small amounts to a TiO_2-based white paint to produce the desired tint.

The naturally-occurring iron oxides have been partly replaced by synthetic products. Synthetic oxides are manufactured from various waste products of the steel industry. Their composition and properties can be closely controlled; this is a special advantage in assuring uniformity, so that a given color can be precisely duplicated time after time. But the natural pigments are still used, especially in primers or undercoats, where color is not so important, and in anti-corrosive paint for bridges and other structures. Natural pigments

White marble everywhere: in the ledges, on the road, in the truck. This mine in Georgia originally produced blocks for buildings and memorials, but now supplies stone for ground calcium carbonate. (Courtesy of Georgia Marble Company.)

cost $250 to $500 per ton, whereas synthetics cost $850 to as much as $1700 per ton. In 1978, natural iron-oxide pigments used in the United States totalled about 78,000 tons, of which 11,000 tons was imported; synthetics totalled 111,000 tons, of which nearly half was imported.

Extending the pigment. Several minerals are used to substitute for a part of the expensive TiO_2 pigment in paint. The most important of these are kaolin, talc, and calcium carbonate. They are especially valuable in water-based paints, to which they add several useful properties besides acting as extenders.

Kaolin, as we saw in the discussion of paper, is brilliant white and readily dispersible in water-based systems. Since it can be provided in the same grain size as the TiO_2—in the range of 0.2 to 0.4 micron—it aids in spacing the TiO_2 particles. The flat platelets of kaolin also contribute to ease of application with the brush. Kaolin has relatively poor resistance to weather and so is used chiefly in interior paints.

Talc, as the term is used in industry, is a light-colored soft rock composed of magnesium-silicate minerals. It grinds to a powder that is brilliant white. Its softness contributes to smooth paint flow. Talc also has good hiding power, resists settling, and aids in dispersion of the pigment. On an exterior surface, it tends to weather to a white powder and thus is a constituent of "self-cleaning" paints. Talc comes from mines in northwestern New York, where it occurs in a complex series of metamorphic rocks. It is also produced in Vermont and California. Besides being used in paint, talc goes into ceramic products such as porcelain and whiteware. The highest grades, imported from Italy, are used in cosmetics—the familiar talcum powder.

The most widely used paint extender is calcium carbonate. No doubt you recognize this as calcite, the mineral of limestone. Until World War II, the dominant source of ground calcium carbonate was chalk—a variety of limestone—from northern Europe. The "white cliffs of Dover" on the English Channel are well-known exposures of this sedimentary material. A relic of a widespread sea of Cretaceous age (135 to 65 million years ago), the chalk is made up of the tiny shells of marine organisms called coccoliths. (It is unrelated to blackboard chalk, which is a manufactured product containing gypsum.) Still used extensively in European paints, chalk is mined in open pits and ground to a powder that is 96 to 99 percent $CaCO_3$. The structure of the minute coccolith shells governs the nature of the material produced, termed "whiting," which is admirably suited for use as an extender.

During World War II, supplies of whiting to the United States were cut off, and the industry in this country turned to deposits of light-colored pure limestone and white marble. These are now the chief sources in North America. Some of the finest grades come from marble. This rock started its existence as limestone, but has been altered—often purified—by heat and internal earth forces. Major deposits occur in Vermont and Georgia. Marble is best known, of course, as fine polished stone for building and memorials, but these uses are under strong competition from other products. Today, most marble producers have partly or completely abandoned the stone market in favor of producing ground calcium carbonate. This material acts as a white pigment in paint and is valued in exterior applications because of brightness, weather resistance, and ease of washing. It is also used as a filler in plastics, rubber, and even paper.

A substance called precipitated calcium carbonate, or PCC, competes with the natural product. It is made in several ways; one of these consists simply of calcining limestone or marble to produce lime and carbon dioxide, purifying each of these fractions, and then recombining them.

In a recent year, the U.S. paint industry consumed 135,000 tons of kaolin, 178,000 tons of talc, and 250,000 tons of calcium carbonate. Predominance of the last of these rests not only on its valuable properties but also on an economic factor: it is abundant and relatively inexpensive.

8.

Two Industries with Problems

The Florida Phosphates

Food and phosphorus. Raising enough food to feed the world's growing population would seem to be a matter of concern to the agricultural rather than the mineral industry. It is certainly up to the world's farmers and ranchers. But crops will not grow without fertilizers. To achieve the yields needed, farmers must replace the soil's supply of phosphorus (as well as nitrogen and potassium) that is depleted each year by plant uptake. The immense amounts required can be provided only by rocks from the earth's crust. The mining and processing of phosphates has developed into a major mineral industry.

Phosphorus, a word of Greek origin, means "light-bearer"; it refers to the element's ability to generate visible light (phosphorescence). The term "life-bearer" might be more appropriate, because phosphorus is essential to all forms of life; for example, it is present in the calcium phosphate of bones and teeth. Phosphorus in the soil stimulates early root development, hastens crop maturity, and provides winter hardiness. The supply must be continuously replenished.

Phosphorus for fertilizers is derived mostly from sedimentary rocks of various types, collectively termed *phosphate rock*. This material is insoluble, and its phosphorus cannot be used by plants; so it must be chemically processed to yield soluble compounds for plant food.

This country is fortunate in having large resources of phosphate rock. It is produced in Idaho and Wyoming, in Tennessee, and in North Carolina. But 80 percent of U.S. production, which amounts to more than one-third of the world's total output, comes from the state of Florida. A

Florida phosphate rock, locally called "matrix." It is really a phosphatic gravel. Large fragment below knife is bone of the manatee, or "sea cow."

typical year's production from that state is about 40 million tons. Twelve companies mine and process phosphate rock there, and several others are expected to join them. The Florida industry has a unique and perplexing set of problems.

The Florida deposits. About 2,800 square miles of flat land in central Florida, east of Tampa, is underlain at shallow depth by a bed of gravelly sediment that is rich in calcium phosphate. The mineral of interest is a variety of apatite, but this is no place to look for museum-grade specimens, as the apatite occurs in sand-size grains and earthy pebbles, gray or tan in color, which are mixed with clay and ordinary quartz sand. This deposit was laid down in the sea, where the waters were shallow and the sediments were tumbled about and reworked by waves and currents. Thus, the only fossils found are hard and resistant. They include sharks' teeth—many of which are sharp and wicked-looking—and pieces of bone that came

Mining phosphate rock in Florida. Big dragline dumps phosphatic gravel into a pit, where high-pressure hoses churn it into a water suspension. This is pumped to the processing plant through pipeline at left. (Courtesy of Florida Phosphate Council.)

from the manatee, a marine mammal better known as the "sea cow."

Beneath the ground surface is 20 to 40 feet of loose sand. Next below is the phosphate-bearing gravel, about 20 feet thick. The gravel lies on a sandy, claylike limestone, which contains scattered potato-size nodules of phosphate not concentrated enough to mine. All these sediments were deposited during Miocene to Pliocene time, about 10 million years ago, when the Florida peninsula was covered by the sea.

The material is worked in large open pits. Big excavating machines, called draglines, remove the overburden of sand and dump it into a worked-out section of the pit. Then they scoop up the phosphatic gravel and deposit it in a temporary pit, where hydraulic guns, like super-firehoses, convert it into a slurry. The slurry is pumped by pipeline to the washing and concentrating plant, which may be several miles from the mine. In place of a slurry pipeline, one company has installed a two-way conveyor belt. Another is experimenting with rail transport.

Land. The nature of the phosphate deposit—thin, flat, and widespread—means that mining is a land-consuming operation. It cannot be concentrated in a small area. This fact produced no serious problems from 1888, when the mining started, to the 1950s: population density was light, and the land was not highly valued for other purposes. But Florida—the Sunshine State—has become a center for recreation, tourism, and retirement living. A tremendous influx of people, fleeing urban lifestyles for two weeks or the rest of their lives, has radically changed the situation.

Unregulated open-pit mining leaves behind a "moonscape" of piles of over burden, open ditches, and deep pits. Altogether, about 150,000 acres, or over 240 square miles have been strip-mined. As early as 1949, a few of the more responsible companies voluntarily reclaimed their disturbed acres, and several tracts were landscaped and donated as public parks. Mandatory reclamation, however, was not imposed by the state until 1970; today, it is a standard and continuous part of mining operations. Costs of restoring the land have been greatly reduced by deciding ahead of time the final use to which the reclaimed land will be put, and directing all operations toward that end. Dragline operators are pro-

"Moonscape" left after unregulated phosphate mining in Florida.

vided with charts, or are guided by supervisors, as to where overburden is to be placed, and waste sand from the plants is distributed according to plan. By such means, land is produced that can be used for citrus groves, parks, or lake-dotted

Reclamation of mined land for residential use, Florida phosphate district. (Courtesy of Florida Phosphate Council.)

grassland for cattle. Some companies, indeed, have found that their reclaimed land is an asset and have formed subsidiaries to sell, manage, or farm it.

Unfortunately, large areas disturbed in mining cannot be restored to productive use. This is the result of a peculiarly frustrating waste-disposal problem. At the mill, the crude rock is washed and the phosphate-bearing pebbles and sand are separated from quartz sand and clay. The unwanted sand is washed into a pond, where it settles rapidly; it is returned to the mine area for use in reclamation, and the water is recycled to the mill. The clay, however, comes from the mill in a thick yellow liquid, known as *slime*, which is a suspension of colloidal clay particles in water. Slime defies consolidation. After years of standing, it still has the consistency of chocolate pudding. Hence, it must be stored for an indefinite period. Because of the water content, its volume exceeds that of the phosphate rock removed from the pits, so that simply refilling worked-out pits is inadequate. The slime is held behind earthen dams, which are built above the general level of the surrounding countryside. Thousands of acres must be given over to this usage.

There are some 300 miles of slime-pond dams. A constant hazard is that a dam will give way or that heavy rains will cause an overflow, allowing the slime to pour into natural waterways. This has happened several times, with catastrophic loss of fish life. Stringent state laws have improved the quality of the newer dams, but maintaining safe storage conditions for the slime is a continuing problem. The Florida Phosphate Council, representing the companies, and the U.S. Bureau of Mines are sponsoring research which, it is hoped, will come forth with a technique to settle or dewater the slime and thus make it more readily disposable. It is ironic that this baffling and difficult substance is merely a mixture of two of the earth's most common materials: water and clay.

Still another land-consuming problem faces the industry. After phosphate rock is washed and concentrated in the mill, it goes to a plant for manufacture into phosphoric acid for fertilizer. A waste material from the manufacturing process is gypsum. This "phosphogypsum" is not used at present, as it is impure and physically unlike the natural rock gypsum used in making plaster and wallboard; but it is a potential resource. Some 330 million tons of phosphogypsum are stored in "gyp stacks" on the land surface, and millions of tons are added each year. This material was the subject of an international conference in Florida in November 1980. Topics considered included the possible use of phosphogypsum in agriculture, building, and road construction, as well as purification of the material and better techniques of disposal.

Water. Is there enough water in central Florida to satisfy agriculture, industry, and people?

Until a decade or two ago, the question would not have been asked; water was considered limitless. Today, however, it has become precious. Practically all the water comes from wells, most of which are supplied by the "Floridan aquifer," a layer of water-saturated porous limestone several hundred feet below the surface. Rainfall recharges

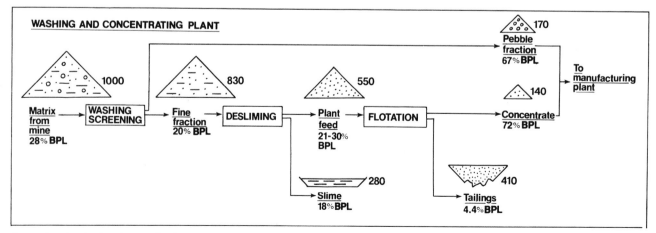

Processing Florida phosphates: what happens to 1,000 tons of mined material. Only 310 tons come out as feed for the manufacturing plant, the remainder being lost as slime and sand. BPL, for "bone phosphate of lime," is a measure of phosphate content.

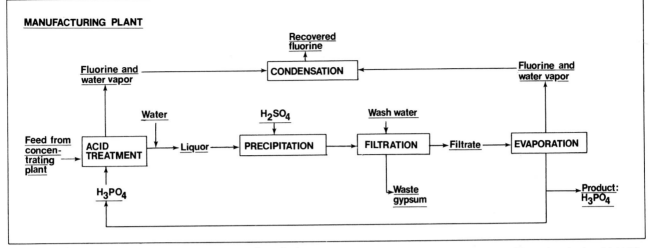

Phosphatic concentrates are converted into phosphoric acid, H_3PO_4, for production of fertilizer. Fluorine is produced as a by-product, and gypsum as waste.

this aquifer via a swampy region north of the phosphate field, but such natural recharge is slow and has not kept pace with withdrawals from wells. In parts of central Florida, the original water table, or upper surface of saturation in the aquifer, has been lowered as much as 60 feet.

The heaviest users of water in most counties are the growers of oranges and other citrus crops. But in Polk County, where phosphate production is centered, about two-thirds of the water is used by industry. To produce one ton of washed and concentrated phosphate rock takes 5,000 gallons of water. Most of this water is used in the slurry pipeline that moves the rock to the mill, in washing the rock, and in the flotation cells by which it is separated from waste. Although some 85 percent of this water is recycled, the remainder is lost, chiefly to evaporation.

Florida receives abundant rainfall, and the crucial question is not so much one of over-all water supply as of preemptive rights: who gets the first right to water use? Communities are constantly expanding, citrus groves must be supplied, and industry requires large quantities of water. Apparently the situation is serious but not critical. State and local authorities will have the water problem with them for a long time to come.

Air. Until the late 1940s, the phosphate industry was confined to mining and concentrating the raw material; the concentrate was shipped elsewhere for manufacture into fertilizer. Then companies began to add their own manufacturing plants, and what had been strictly a mining business turned into a center of chemical processing.

In 1948, farmers in Polk County began to notice a decline in their crop yields, and ranchers' cattle started dying of a mysterious epidemic. It was shortly found that airborne fluorine was the culprit. This active and toxic element prevented normal growth in plants, and, concentrated in forage crops, produced fluorosis—a disease of teeth and bones—in cattle. The source of the fluorine was clearly the newly established phosphate manufacturing plants.

Apatite, the phosphorus-bearing mineral of the Florida deposits, is more correctly known as *fluorapatite*, as it contains 2.5 to 3.5 percent of fluorine. The fluorine must be removed in order to make the phosphate available to plants. Gaseous fluorine was at first emitted to the atmosphere; this was what caused the damage. The problem, which was a new one to the industry and to the state, took some 15 years to correct. Large pieces of equipment, called "scrubbers," were installed at many plants to wash fluorine-bearing air in a pressurized spray of water. Another method of meeting the problem is to combine the fluorine with silica and emit it as harmless silicon fluoride. By 1970, companies were reported to have spent more than $50,000,000 on control devices, and the problem had been overcome. New plants are designed so that air pollution will not occur.

Of recent years, several companies have begun marketing silica-fluorine compounds as a by-product, for use in the aluminum and ceramics industries and in fluoridation of drinking water. Although the amounts produced are modest, this procedure has great potential significance because the Florida phosphates are the largest known source of fluorine in North America. Increased production would markedly affect this country's consumption of fluorspar, 82 percent of which is imported.

Radiation. The fluorapatite of the phosphate deposits contains an average of 0.015 percent (150 parts per million) of uranium oxide, U_3O_8. This occurs not only in the mined material but in a thin zone at the base of the overburden. The U_3O_8 is inactive in the undisturbed beds. But when the overburden is picked up and piled to one side, the radioactive zone is exposed. Solution by rain water may dissolve radioactive material and move it downward into the ground-water system. And the natural radioactivity of the mined material accompanies it to the washing and concentrating plant, through the manufacturing process, and into the final product and the waste materials. The phosphogypsum seems to be exceptionally radioactive, and seepage from the "gyp stacks" may release radioactive substances to the surface and ground waters.

So possible hazards from radiation are the latest developments in the environmental picture. It has not been established that they are serious, but both industry and government are studying the problem.

From the companies' point of view, the picture has a bright side. The U_3O_8 may be separated and concentrated during the manufacturing process and sold as a by-product. It is eventually purchased by utilities to fuel nuclear reactors in power plants. This development got under way only in 1978, but within two years four companies were producing U_3O_8 and at least two others were preparing to do so. A forecast is that by the mid-1980s Florida will be furnishing 15 percent of the nation's requirements for uranium oxide.

Regulation. As a result of its unique set of environmental problems—bringing it into uneasy contact with citrus agriculture, cattle raising, tourism, and urban expansion—the production of Florida phosphates has become one of the most regulated mining industries in the country.

Programs affecting surface mining are now based on five state laws, all enacted in the 1970s: a comprehensive planning act, an environmental land and water management act, a local government comprehensive planning act, a water

resources act, and a severance tax law. Certain county and local ordinances add to the list.

A company seeking to start a new mine must conform to a complex set of permits and regulations. At least 25 studies, reports, and surveys—all time-consuming, and all expensive—must be made before mining may start. At the federal level, the Environmental Protection Agency and the Army Corps of Engineers may be involved. At the state level are requirements of the Division of State Planning, the Department of Environmental Regulation, a water management district, and the Department of Natural Resources. And at the county level, zoning approval must be obtained for a master plan, a development order, an operating permit, and a building permit. Altogether, a company may expect to spend many months and between $1.5 million and $3.75 million for the required clearances before mining may start.

Large reserves of phosphate remain to be mined, and the industry is thriving despite its problems. With cooperation between producers and the various levels of government, the industry should continue for a long time to contribute essential products to the economy and to figure largely in the economic life of Florida.

Asbestos and Health

Asbestos is a general name for a group of fibrous minerals. About 99 percent of the world's commercial production consists of just three minerals. *Chrysotile* (sometimes called "white asbestos") is by far the most important. As we saw in Chapter 3, it is a fibrous form of the mineral serpentine, a hydrous silicate of magnesium. Chrysotile is mined in several countries and over the years has accounted for 90 to 95 percent of world production. It is the only asbestos mineral mined in North America. *Crocidolite* ("blue asbestos") is a complex silicate of sodium, magnesium, and iron. It was mined in Western Australia until 1966 but is now produced only in South Africa. It makes up about 3 percent of present world production. *Amosite* ("brown asbestos") is a fibrous form of the mineral cummingtonite, an iron-magnesium silicate. Mined in the Transvaal area of South Africa, it makes up about 2 percent of present world output.

Veinlets of chrysotile asbestos in dark serpentine rock, with separated fibers in foreground. Enlarged about three times. (Courtesy of Johns-Manville Canada Inc.)

Hundreds of uses for these fibrous minerals have been developed. Among the products in which they are used are asbestos-cement panels and pipes, floor tile, brake linings, clutch facings, insulation for ships' boilers and pipes, textiles, chemical filter cloth, and packings. From 1946 to 1973, asbestos was used in coatings that could be

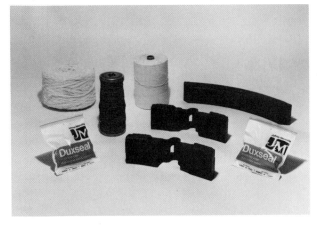

A few products made with chrysotile asbestos. The yarns are used in textiles, the three black forms are locomotive brake linings, and the envelopes contain sealing compound. (Courtesy of Johns-Manville Canada Inc.)

sprayed onto walls in lieu of plaster. In all, some 30 million tons have been used in the United States since 1900.

The health problem. Prolonged breathing of air laden with asbestos dust may cause lung disease. Extremely fine fibers enter the air-cleaning cells of the lungs and cannot be expelled. Fibers that remain in the lungs cause certain biochemical reactions, leading to three significant lung diseases: (1) *asbestosis,* a scarring of the tissue, which decreases the lungs' ability to function properly and is similar to coal miners' "black lung"; (2) *mesothelioma,* a cancer of the lining of the lung (and also of the digestive tract); and (3) *lung cancer.* Unfortunately, a disease may appear many years after exposure to asbestos dust, by which time a cure may not be possible.

In the past, persons who worked with asbestos or its products in factories, shipyards, shops, and other industrial sites showed high mortality from asbestosis, mesothelioma, and lung cancer. These "trades" workers were generally exposed during their working careers to all three asbestiform minerals as they moved from job to job; some of the products they used were made of two types of asbestos. Since the materials used in the asbestos trades are diverse and come from a variety of sources, medical studies of trades workers usually cannot be used to pinpoint damage from one or another of the asbestos minerals. These studies merely show that years of breathing dusty fiber-laden air in the workplace is likely to damage the lungs. With government encouragement, the industry has corrected once-dangerous conditions in factory and shop. Government standards now allow no more than two of the fine fibers per cubic centimeter of air. It was the lack of such standards before the 1960s that allowed many asbestos workers to contract cancer that is only now showing up or will appear in the future.

The risky minerals. Is dust from all three asbestos minerals equally dangerous? The question may be answered by medical studies made of the men involved with the mining and milling of these minerals. These studies show that miners and millers of chrysotile in Canada and northern Italy have mortality rates from lung cancer and mesothelioma that differ very little from those of the general population. On the other hand, studies

The Jeffrey asbestos mine, Quebec, Canada. In operation since 1881, it is now more than a mile across and 1,150 feet deep. (Courtesy of Johns-Manville Canada Inc.)

of South African miners and millers of crocidolite show a high incidence of mesothelioma. A crocidolite mine in Western Australia was closed in 1966 after miners and millers showed an extreme mortality pattern—even though they were exposed to the mineral for only short periods of time, averaging 8 to 9 months. Crocidolite has been essentially banned in Britain, but is used in the United States to make asbestos-cement pipe. Available data indicate that amosite may be dangerous, but a full study has not been made.

It is clear that exposure to chrysotile dust is dangerous only if heavy and prolonged; there is also evidence that lung cancer is higher in workers who smoke cigarettes. (Some companies will not hire smokers.) Occasional or slight exposure poses no threat. Crocidolite, on the other hand, is dangerous, and possibly amosite is as well. These

facts would seem to be the logical starting point for handling the "asbestos problem." The medical community, however, does not see things this way; it treats all asbestos the same, and so do the EPA and other regulatory agencies of the U.S. government. One effect of this policy has been to create alarm and confusion on the part of the general public. Indeed, public concern about the "asbestos hazard" has at times approached hysteria. People using hair dryers have been frightened because the dryers contain asbestos insulation. In Arizona, a mobile-home park was relocated because it was found to be situated on the site of a former chrysotile mill. A crushed-stone quarry in Maryland was cited when the rock was found to contain a fraction of 1 percent of chrysotile. When it was revealed that asbestos wall coatings had been used in school buildings across the country, local school boards were urged to have this material ripped out—though this procedure would of course create dust, the very substance that has been found to be hazardous.

Even the minuscule amounts of dust liberated in the normal use of automobile brake linings—which contain chrysotile—have come under suspicion. But the dust (what there is of it) is not asbestos: the heat and pressure generated when the brakes are applied causes a change in composition to a harmless variety of the mineral olivine. Nevertheless, one company that manufactures brake linings has felt it necessary to spend many millions of dollars on substitutes—so far without finding a satisfactory product.

The health and regulatory agencies not only treat all asbestos minerals the same, but they define as dangerous all airborne particles that are more than three times as long as wide. By this definition, the mineral tremolite, which occurs with talc in some commercial deposits, must be labelled "asbestos," although there is little evidence that tremolite is hazardous. Even the talc and vermiculite industries have suffered from "guilt by association." In fact, under the definition cited, "asbestos" minerals are present in a great variety of rocks and mining environments.

Regulation and banishment. In 1979, the Environmental Protection Agency announced plans to regulate all aspects of the asbestos consumer-products industry. It has also stated that it intends eventually to impose a ban on most uses of asbestos in this country, irrespective of mineral type. It is as though a government agency, having determined that poison ivy is undesirable and even dangerous, decided not only to ban this plant but also Boston ivy, English ivy, Virginia creeper, pachysandra, and honeysuckle, as well as mountain laurel, which is called "ivy" in some parts of the country.

Should a total ban go into effect, this will of course have serious consequences on the asbestos industry. That such an effect may have shown up already is suggested by figures relating new construction to the consumption of asbestos. In the 9 years preceding 1977, the value of new construction and the use of asbestos went up and down together; in 1977, however, construction values were on the rise but asbestos consumption dropped. This is almost certainly a reflection of public concern about the health problem.

In July 1980, the Environmental Protection Agency and the Consumer Product Safety Commission sponsored a national workshop in Washington, D.C., on substitutes for asbestos. Users of asbestos, and potential suppliers of substitute products, were on hand. Four conclusions emerged. First, there are or soon will be substitutes for asbestos in practically all its applications—in the form of ceramic fibers, glass fibers, steel wool, cellulose, vinyl, epoxy resin, or other materials. Second, few of the substitutes will be as good as the asbestos they replace. Third, they will cost more. Finally, some may themselves be hazardous. If a total ban on asbestos takes place, it is clear that consumers will be paying more for products of poorer quality. The label "asbestos-free" on a product will satisfy the law and will presumably compensate the consumer for the factors just mentioned.

In sum, the term "asbestos," as rationally used, refers to three minerals. Exposure to dust from one of these, crocidolite, is dangerous, and warrants complete elimination from commerce. As to the second, amosite, the evidence is inconclusive. Exposure to the third and by far the most widely used asbestos mineral, chrysotile, does not lead to abnormal health risks unless it is breathed in high concentrations for long periods of time. Occasional use of the many products that contain chrysotile presents no health hazard. Imposing a wholesale ban on this versatile and extremely useful material does not seem justified.

9.

Blast it Out and Break it Up (But Not in My Neighborhood)

We mentioned in Chapter 1 this country's vast appetite for concrete, the building material that consists of a little cement and a lot of aggregate. Annual production of aggregate approaches 2 billion tons. About half is crushed stone, and half is sand and gravel. Supplies are adequate at most places, processing is not difficult, and demand is seemingly endless. It appears that the construction-aggregates industry should have an easy time. But

certain problems beset it. The most serious of these are neither geological nor technical, but social and political.

A Case of Controlled Chaos

To the casual observer, operations at a typical stone quarry and processing plant must appear chaotic, but in reality they are closely controlled. Down on the quarry floor, a power shovel loads trucks with chunks of rock that were brought down from the quarry face by yesterday's blast. The trucks rumble across the quarry and dump the stone into the maw of a crusher, which breaks it into pieces no larger than 8 inches across. From here the stone is moved by conveyor belt up to the plant on the surface level. This consists of a maze of crushing, washing, and screening equipment from which emerge a dozen or more grades of stone, from the size of your fist down to that of small pebbles. Each of these grades accumulates in a cone-shaped pile built below an inclined conveyor belt that brings the material from the plant. From these piles the stone is loaded out by truck to the road-building job or other point of use.

Stone also goes by belt to a ready-mix concrete plant that is right next door, and the finer grades are conveyed to an adjacent hot-mix asphalt plant that produces "blacktop" for streets and roads.

While all this is going on, scrapers and trucks are at work ahead of quarrying, removing soil and weathered rock from the desired stone. On the upper surface of the cleared-off ledge, a few yards back from the quarry face, a crew drills rows of

Drilling holes in preparation for blasting at a limestone quarry. Detonating explosives in these holes will bring down several thousand tons of broken rock. (Courtesy of National Limestone Institute.)

A blast at a stone quarry. (Courtesy of National Limestone Institute.)

holes in the rock. These will be charged with explosives for blasting down a fresh supply of stone when the shovel has cleaned up the present one.

To the superintendent of operations, who manages the whole scene from a glass-enclosed cubicle mounted on stilts at a good vantage point, each activity has a purpose, and all are monitored to assure that they work smoothly together. The appearance of chaos is entirely deceptive. The material produced may be devoid of glamour, but it is indispensable to the growth of the community.

Growing with the Community

Let us give such an operation a name and a history. In 1935, when the Agmix Stone Company went into business, its quarry was 15 miles from the center of a medium-sized town and 10 miles from the outskirts. Its only neighbor was a farmer down the road. In the post-war boom the town expanded, and suburbs appeared on its outer fringes. Farms were converted into residential areas; because there were trees and some rolling land out toward the Agmix area, this section was in special demand. Eventually the suburbs reached and bypassed the Agmix property, and now they surround it. Beyond the company's yet-unquarried property, instead of cornfields there are expensive

homes and a golf course. Quiet paved streets have replaced the country roads of earlier days. Schools, churches, and shopping centers have sprung up.

If you imagine that Agmix Stone Company is not accepted with enthusiasm by its new neighbors, you are quite correct. The quarry is scarcely an esthetic addition to a wealthy suburb. Indeed, the site can be described as a bad scene: dusty, noisy, and all too visible. There is a big hole in the ground, which is getting wider all the time. There are immense piles of rock material, and a complicated cluster of machinery, all presided over by rough-looking men in hard hats. Every day or two, another blast rattles windows. Big trucks roar in and out using suburban streets. Regularly the town fathers are served with demands from nearby residents that this intolerable nuisance be forced to move away.

Realizing all this, Agmix has tried to act as a good corporate citizen. Why shouldn't it, after all? The company has done good business by supplying the community with an essential material: half the concrete in the county was made with Agmix aggregate. So the company landscapes its property, adds a fence to keep youngsters from the quarry's hazards, and replaces its office shack with

Broken limestone after a blast, ready for trucking to primary crusher.
(Courtesy of National Limestone Institute.)

a modest but attractive building. It agrees to schedule blasts as infrequently as possible and at pre-announced times, and to minimize noise and shock waves—especially air shock, which, it turns out, causes more complaints than ground vibration. The company further agrees to operate its trucks only at certain hours and on designated streets. It waters the haul roads in the quarry to suppress dust. It contributes to local charities and supports a softball team, the Agmix Aggies.

Nevertheless, the company's days at this site are numbered. Even though it owns enough land for five more years of operation, there is no guarantee that it will be allowed to use it. At present the property is zoned "industrial," and thus available for quarrying; but at tonight's meeting of the county zoning commission the property may be reclassified as "commercial," "residential," or "recreational." If this happens, quarrying becomes what is called a "nonconforming use," and the company will have 12 months or the like in which to close down. The situation is ironic indeed. A community that has been able to grow at will, largely because of cheap, close-in construction materials, is now in conflict with the industry that made that growth possible.

Of course the management of Agmix has seen this situation coming for a long time and has taken appropriate steps. A tract of land has been purchased that has a large supply of good stone at shallow depth, is without close neighbors, and is adjacent to a highway. Inevitably, this site is well out in the country, and transportation costs will be

Loading limestone after a blast. (Courtesy of National Limestone Institute.)

high, relative to the cost of the material. So contractors in the city and suburbs will have to pay more than formerly for aggregate. But the intolerable nuisance will have disappeared from the prosperous suburb. The old quarry is to be converted into a nice clean industrial park, where light industry will be welcome to pursue its business quietly in neatly landscaped buildings.

Zoned Out or Nullified

Being "zoned out of business" is by no means an imaginary situation. It has happened repeatedly, for example, on Long Island east of New York City. Here the desired material is sand and gravel. Extraction of this material is much like that of stone, but no blasting and little crushing are necessary. The product is just removed, washed, and screened into size grades. The number of gravel pits on Long Island decreased from 27 in 1967 to 7 in 1974, mainly because producers exhausted their supplies and were unable to expand or relocate, owing to prohibitive zoning practices. No new sand and gravel operation has been allowed in Nassau County (Long Island) since about 1960, although in theory the local laws permit it. (From the end of World War II to 1970, Nassau and

neighboring Suffolk counties were the fastest-growing counties in the United States, more than quadrupling their population. Eighty-five percent of the new housing in Nassau County was land-consuming single-family houses. No wonder the aggregate business was squeezed out!)

The experience of one producer is instructive. The company had long operated a large pit at Port Washington on Long Island's north shore. This locality is 18.5 miles from Battery Park on the southern tip of Manhattan Island. All of the gravel was moved cheaply by barge. The company decided to move when the deposit was nearly exhausted, and no more favorably zoned land was available. After an extensive geological search, the firm relocated near Plainsboro, New Jersey. This point is 40 miles from Battery Park. The aggregate must be moved 25 miles by rail, and then transferred into barges at a loading facility that had to be specially built.

Aggregate from distant sources such as Plainsboro is available in the greater New York area, but it costs more. The average delivered price for sand, for example, rose from $2.50 per ton in 1969 to about $4.50 in 1975—an increase of 80 percent. Thus, a builder needing 100,000 tons of sand for a shopping center or housing project paid $200,000 more for it in 1975 than he would have paid just 6 years before.

Another problem arises when good deposits of aggregate—sand and gravel in a natural terrace along a river, for example—are sealed off from use because a highway or a housing project is built on them. Thus, the same expansion that increases the

The structure houses the primary crusher. Stone then goes by covered conveyor to plant beyond quarry for further crushing and screening. (Courtesy of National Limestone Institute.)

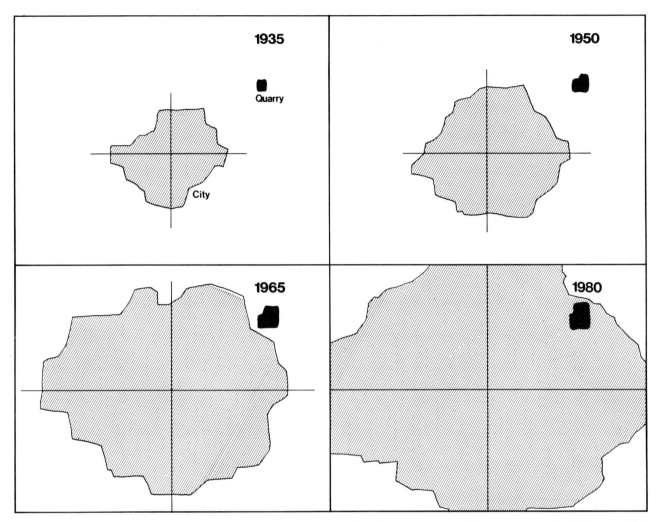

1935
■ Quarry
City

1950

1965

1980

A crushed-stone quarry, well out in the country in 1935, is now inside the city limits. Neighbors object to its unsightliness, noise, dust, and truck traffic.

demand for aggregate may cover the land that could supply it. This problem, which has been referred to as "cultural nullification," has been anticipated at a few places. In the San Gabriel Valley, California, not far from Los Angeles, lawsuits sparked by zoning have resulted in the designation of "natural resource districts," that is, lands reserved for expansion of sand and gravel operations. The provincial government of Ontario has passed similar legislation. But, in general, problems of this type tend to be met on an ad-hoc, emergency basis, the final decisions resting with local planning boards or city councils. Naturally enough, each of these bodies sees the problem from its own point of view, and it is politically unpopular to advocate that state authority should supersede local autonomy.

It is interesting that some of the strongest voices urging state or regional planning in regard to resources of aggregate come from the companies themselves. These companies are alarmed because in the same urban corridors where excavation is barred the suburbs spread apace, thus nullifying more and more potential future production. The Ontario legislation setting aside mineral-resource areas, noted above, was enacted at the behest of the province's producing companies. Desirable as such programs are, it is likely that for the most part we will continue to "muddle through" on a local (and increasingly expensive) basis.

Sequential Land Use

New lives for mined-out land. About 3 miles from the Civic Center of Denver, Colorado, is a tract of

A quarry and its neighbors. The rock is granite, the locality Atlanta. (U.S. Bureau of Mines.)

roughly 100 acres that has had a more interesting history than most pieces of real estate. Situated on a terrace of the South Platte River, the site was open, undisturbed *grazing land* until the 1920s. Later, it was acquired by an aggregates company which operated a sand-and-gravel pit on the site. Thus, it became *mineral-bearing land*. By the end of World War II the gravel was depleted, and the site was a broad empty pit. Its third incarnation came in the 1950s, when the pit became valuable as a site for trash disposal—*a sanitary landfill*. By 1960 the pit was filled, the fill was compacted, and the tract was graded for its fourth and present purpose: the site of the Denver Coliseum and parking areas. Today, in short, it is valuable *urban real estate*. Motorists passing the site on Interstate Highway 70 see no evidence of the three useful lives that preceded the present one.

From this sort of accidental or casually planned sequential land use, it is only a step to long-range planning. Nowadays, urban planners and responsible producers of aggregate take it for granted that land currently productive of gravel or stone will ultimately serve some other purpose. Indeed, companies have found that it is often possible to sell rehabilitated land for considerably more than they paid for it, even though they have removed the aggregate in the meantime. At a reclamation project in the San Fernando Valley of southern California, a 71-acre pit has been used for disposal of trash since 1961 and will continue to be used until 1983. When filled and leveled, the property will be highly valuable real estate. At another pit in the Valley, waste disposal began in 1953 and the

Hedge along property line screens active sand-and-gravel pit from public view. (Courtesy of American Aggregates Corporation.)

pit was filled to the original ground level by 1970. The property sold for about $21,000 per acre.

In the 1950s, the federal government constructed a multiple-building high-rise housing project in St. Louis. From the start it was beset with social problems, and in 1972 it was adjudged to have been a failure. In the nation's largest demolition job, more than 25 buildings were razed. The debris, of course, had to be taken away. But what do you do with 500,000 tons of shattered apartment houses? Fortunately, just 10 miles from the site was a 200-foot-deep quarry, which could be used for "clean fill" if the affluent surrounding community would give its approval. It took 11 formal hearings, spread over 15 months, to persuade the council and concerned citizens that the proposed landfill would consist of inert brick, plaster, and concrete, rather than noxious garbage. The final agreement included numerous restrictions, especially to the end that only authorized dumping was allowed. A maximum time limit was also placed on the operation.

Not all such proposals are successful. In the early 1970s it was suggested that a large, worked-out sandstone quarry in northern Ohio was suitable for a landfill, which was badly needed in the area. A favorable factor was that the site was underlain by shale, an impervious rock that would not allow the escape of noxious substances into the ground water. The proposal was approved by the state environmental agency, the state health authorities, and the county commissioners, but met unyielding opposition from local residents. So the old quarry remains open to the sky, awaiting a new use.

Lakes on the landscape. In the east-central United States, many deposits of sand and gravel are below the water table; thus, after extraction of the material, the area is a pond or lake. Advance planning, which allows landscaping to be done while the sand and gravel are being removed, is standard operating procedure for most companies. At a site in Indianapolis, for example, the

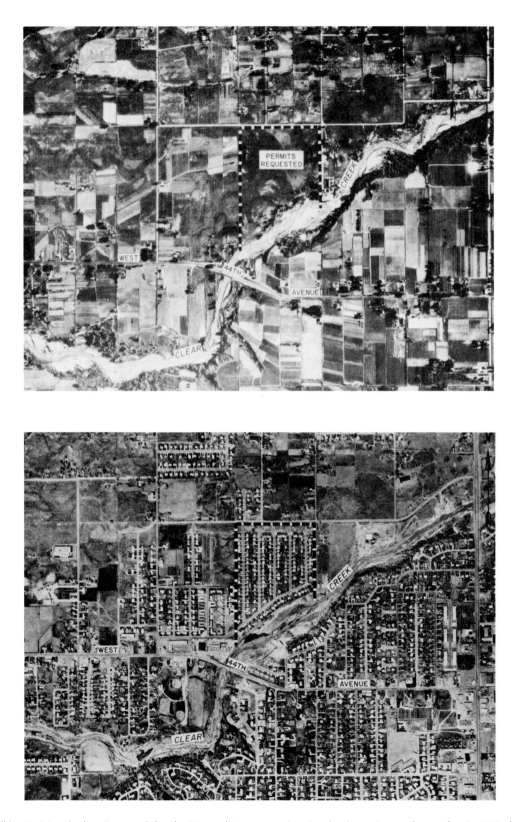

"Cultural nullification" in suburban Denver, Colorado. Upper photo was taken in 1938. Landowner's repeated requests for a permit to remove sand and gravel from the indicated area were denied because of protests by nearby residents. The owner then sold the property to a housing developer. Lower photo, taken in 1965, shows same tract after houses were built. The sand and gravel will never be extracted. (U.S. Bureau of Mines.)

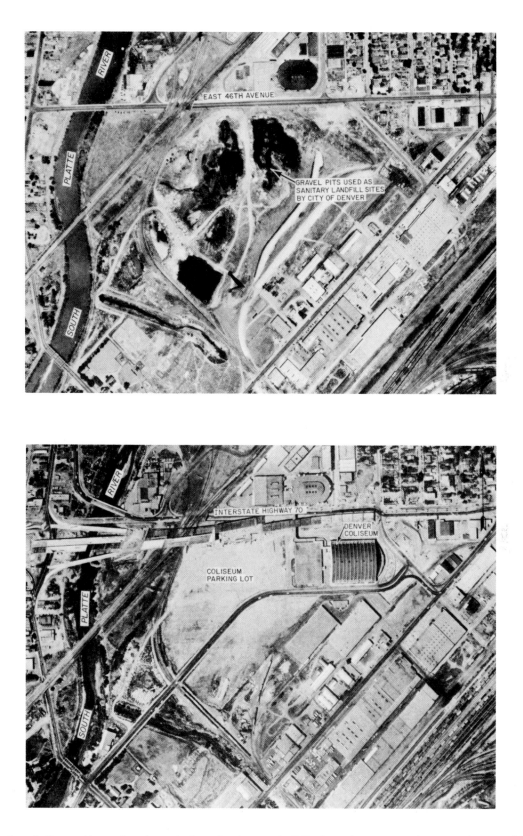

Sequential land use in Denver. Upper photo is an air view taken in 1948, after the tract had been depleted of its sand and gravel and was being used by the city for disposal of solid waste. Lower photo, taken in 1962, shows the same area after conversion to useful urban property. (U.S. Bureau of Mines.)

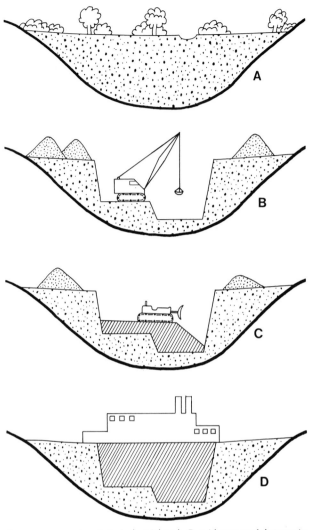

From open country, A, to industrial park, D, with two useful stages in between. (U.S. Geological Survey.)

material was removed by a suction dredge and pumped to a preliminary screening unit that screened out excess sand. The coarser fraction was taken to the plant by conveyor belt. The excess sand was distributed to make attractive building sites along the lake shore when dredging was completed.

Stone, as well as sand and gravel, may be extracted from deposits that lie below the water table if the quarry is kept dry by pumping. Lakes that form after quarrying and pumping cease are scenic additions to the landscape. In Columbus, Ohio, the margin of a lake in a long-abandoned limestone quarry is the site of a complex of offices, apartments, and commercial buildings, all with recreational facilities close by. Lone Star Park, a

400-acre "planned business community" near Dallas, occupies the site of a former cement plant. It focuses on a lake which fills the old limestone quarry that supplied the plant.

Trading stone for space. Montclair State College, a unit of the New Jersey educational system, is situated at the foot of a steep, wooded rocky ridge known as First Watchung Mountain. In 1960, the college was in need of space for expansion. Sixteen acres of its 75-acre campus were of no use because they lay on the mountain slope and were underlain at shallow depth by dense hard basalt. This rock, a heavy dark lava, is known in the crushed-stone industry as "traprock." Just next door to the campus was a large quarry, which had been operated for many years by a producer of traprock for the New York-New Jersey market. The company's reserve of unquarried stone was diminishing, and new supplies were being sought.

Early in 1961, a contract was signed between the state of New Jersey and the traprock company, under which the company agreed to remove some 3 million tons of stone from the college's mountainous tract and to leave about 16 acres of level, graded ground. Although the basic idea was simple, indeed obvious, it was complicated by a variety of problems, all of which had to be settled ahead of time. The entrances to the college and the quarry were in different communities. The property was crossed by, or adjacent to, a high-tension power line, a primary water main, a 36-inch gas line, and the Erie-Lackawanna Railroad. Liability insurance was furnished by the company. Even though as much as 18,000 tons of stone was brought down at every blast from quarry faces 60 feet high, no appreciable damage was done to the college buildings just outside the quarry. More than 150 complaints were received from nearby residents, but their cogency lost force when it was found that 80 of them came from only four persons and 34 more from five others. All complaints were settled without litigation.

In spite of environmental problems and hazards, the job was successfully completed a year ahead of schedule. A major reason for the success of the project was its inherent good sense: the college needed the space, the company needed the stone. Furthermore, students and faculty of the college, as well as area residents, were kept informed from

Demolition of the Pruitt-Igoe housing project, St. Louis. Debris was trucked to an abandoned quarry. (U.S. Department of Housing and Urban Development.)

the beginning, and a community meeting was held at which the entire project was carefully detailed. The fact that it had the backing of the state of New Jersey undoubtedly helped. Nevertheless, the whole operation was an example of good advance planning and general community acceptance.

Take the gravel and run—with our blessing. An interesting project got under way in 1979 on a 70-acre tract some 20 miles west of Cincinnati. Two companies were involved: a producer of aggregate and a developer of real estate. The aggregate company contracted to remove and stockpile the topsoil, and then to extract sand and gravel down to a grade specified by the developer. About 22 acres of the tract were taken up by the gravel-processing plant. The remaining 48 acres were to be landscaped by the developer and to become the site of 155 residences. The gravel company was in the happy position of not having to reclaim the property. The development company inherited a custom-contoured, ready-made area on which to build.

The Aggregate Facts of Life

We have seen that the major markets for concrete aggregate are the big cities, where the construction is. We have also mentioned, but not specifically identified, another fact: aggregate, being a bulky, heavy, low-cost commodity, cannot profitably be shipped very far. A general rule in the industry is that the selling price per ton of stone, sand, or gravel is approximately doubled by 20 miles of transportation. So cities cannot obtain their aggregate from some far-off pit or quarry where no one will be disturbed. They have to obtain it locally. In this chapter we have seen examples of both friction and cooperation between company and community that arise from this simple fact.

A second fact is geologic rather than economic. Construction aggregates, like other earth materials, are sporadically distributed. A company cannot count on finding sound stone or clean sand

Royal Botanical Gardens, Hamilton, Ontario, Canada. This is a former limestone quarry: ledges can be seen in left foreground. (Courtesy of Royal Botanical Gardens.)

Reclaimed and landscaped gravel pit in western Ohio. Gravel extraction continues in right background. (Courtesy of American Aggregates Corporation.)

Exchanging stone for flat ground. An aggregates company removed 3 million tons of stone from the property of Montclair State College, New Jersey, leaving 16 acres of flat ground for expansion of the college. Campus buildings are in background. (Courtesy of Houdaille Construction Materials, Inc..)

and gravel by the millions of tons just anywhere. So relocating involves a great deal more than merely moving machinery to a new site. Months of geologic study and core drilling are commonly required, as was the case with the erstwhile gravel producer on Long Island who finally relocated in New Jersey. Added to the geologic factor are various environmental requirements. Indeed, one operator has remarked feelingly, "A producer with a pit he can turn into a living wage is one of the children of God." Everything considered, we believe this to be a reasonable statement.

10.

Looking into the 80s

The United States adds more than 4,200 people to its population every day. This is 29,000 per week, 120,000 per month, one and a half million every year. From the mineral industries' standpoint, the good news is that these new citizens will need its products. But they will also need air, water, space, and recreational facilities. These two needs may conflict. Indeed, the mineral industries as a whole are meeting the same environmental problems on the national scene that producers of aggregate have long known at the community level. Against this background of unrelenting population growth we consider several factors relating to future mineral production.

Mineral Deposits in Limbo

Until the middle of this century, it was taken for granted that if a company discovered a valuable new mineral deposit, it could, under long-established legal rules, proceed to mine it. Today the situation is altogether different. If the company is permitted to mine, it will almost certainly be under tight constraints; often, it will not be allowed to mine a new deposit at all. "Limbo" is defined as a condition of neglect or oblivion. A phosphate deposit in California is in limbo; a vermiculite deposit in Virginia has finally escaped it. We will look at each of these.

Phosphates in a national forest, with condors. A large deposit of phosphate rock is known to exist at Pine Mountain in Los Padres National Forest, southern California. It occurs as a bed of sedimentary rock, 90 feet thick; along with other strata of Miocene age, it is exposed along a hill slope. In 1964, a mining company secured a 2-year prospecting permit from the Bureau of Land Management and in 1966 a 3-year renewal. After proving

the presence of some 80 million tons of accessible ore of minable grade, the company applied for a mining permit in 1969. In 1981—12 years later—the application was still being considered. No permit had been issued.

Deposits of phosphates on public lands are administered under the Mineral Leasing Act of 1920. The company complied with all regulations of this act. The U.S. Geological Survey examined the site and all prospecting data and stated that the company was entitled to a permit to mine. Then, in 1970, came the National Environmental Policy Act, followed shortly by the requirement of an Environmental Impact Statement (EIS) for all such proposed activities as the phosphate mine. The Bureau of Land Management issued a draft EIS in 1971 and a final EIS in 1976. The Bureau held public hearings and solicited comments from other agencies, private organizations, and the general public.

Strong opposition developed, which centered on two facts. The first is that the proposed mine would be on the public domain, near the center of a large block of national forest land. The total lease, 2,434 acres, is small compared to the area of the Los Padres National Forest and involves no park or wilderness area. Nevertheless, the right of a private company to use mineral resources from public lands to make a profit was strongly contested. The second fact cited in opposition is that the proposed mine is only 15 miles from the Sespe Condor Sanctuary and lies in the flying and soaring corridor of the California condor. This bird has been declared a rare and endangered species.

The company proposed to disturb about 500 acres—20 percent of the total lease—in mining, plant operation, and road construction, and to reclaim all disturbed land. It showed that water pollution would be minimal, soil erosion slight,

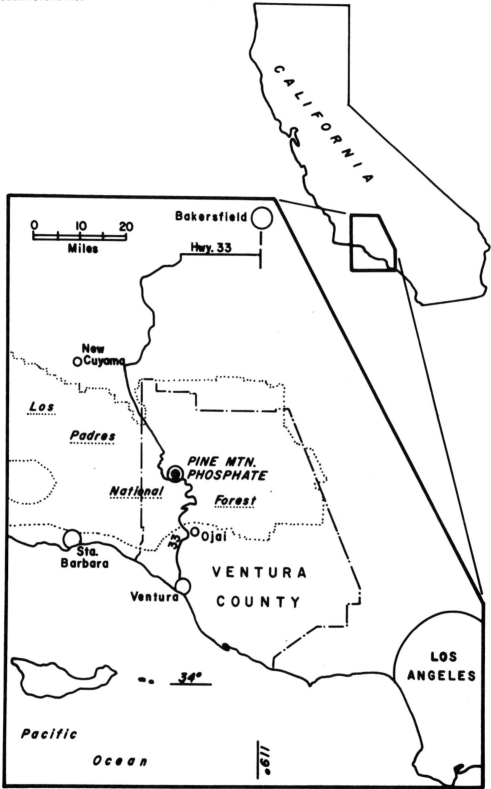

A mineral deposit in limbo. Mining of phosphate rock at Pine Mountain, California, has been prevented because the deposit lies within a national forest. It is also on the flyway of the California condor, an endangered species. (Courtesy of United States Gypsum Company.)

and waste disposal readily handled. But, interestingly, objections to the mine did not focus on these matters. Rather, the company found its application considered in the light of philosophies of land use and special aspects of wildlife conservation. In the last analysis, the problem is one of ethics and preference: the need for recreational use of undeveloped public lands versus the need for an earth-derived mineral resource. The length of time that has elapsed without a disposition of this case, and the amount of money and professional effort that have been invested in it, illustrate the difficulty of making such decisions.

Vermiculite vs. historic countryside. In the early 1970s, a mining company discovered a major deposit of vermiculite a few feet below the surface of rolling farm lands in Louisa County, Virginia. The deposit lies about 50 miles northwest of Richmond and 90 miles southwest of Washington, D.C. If developed, it would add a major new source of vermiculite to the country's two producing districts: the Libby mine in Montana, discussed in Chapter 6, and a few smaller mines in South Carolina. All property is privately owned. In 1974, the company requested a lease and announced that it hoped to start mining in 1980. These actions stirred intense controversy.

Interest in Louisa County centers in the Green Springs area of prosperous and historic farms. (Green Springs is said to get its name from the lush greenness of the fields, owing to the vermiculite-rich soil holding moisture unusually well.) To allow mining, the land would have to be rezoned from agricultural to industrial. The decision on rezoning rested with the county board of supervisors, who found that land-owners were sharply divided: some wished to lease their land for mining, others emphatically did not. Proponents pointed out that vermiculite is a soft mineral that will not require blasting and will not leave unsightly cliffs or ledges but a surface that can readily be restored to productive use. Opponents cited barren "strip mines" at the company's property in South Carolina—in spite of the fact that this mining was done decades before the advent of environmental constraints and in disregard of the fact that the company now regularly reclaims its mined lands. After more than 2 years of deadlocked board meetings, public hearings, lawsuits, and court orders, the board of

supervisors voted in favor of rezoning and mining.

In 1974, the U.S. Department of the Interior designated the Green Springs area a "national historic district." Under this ruling, the Department would accept "scenic easements" from land-owners, binding the government and the land-owners to do nothing to alter the landscape. In August 1980, however, a federal judge reversed this designation. In the meantime, a small mining company—not the one that was first involved—started operations, and Virginia has now joined the list of vermiculite-producing states. The future of large-scale mining in the area remains in doubt.

Much of the controversy in the Green Springs area has not centered on practical matters of land reclamation and the like, but simply on "what will inevitably be an intrusive and disruptive development in the historic district," as opponents put it. The entire story points up once again how difficult it is to reach a compromise between those who advocate the *status quo* and those who wish to alter it, however carefully, by extraction of mineral resources.

Alternatives

Going underground. Producers of crushed stone for urban markets must be situated close to point of use, but must not use too much land or degrade the environment. Some producers have found it possible and profitable to turn to underground mining. If geologic conditions are favorable and good stone is available within reasonable reach, a producer is faced with a fairly clear-cut choice. Disadvantages include higher costs, the necessity of leaving about 30 percent of the rock in the ground as supporting pillars, the possibility of encountering underground water, and limits on the size of equipment that can be used. But these are offset by several advantages: year-round operation, independent of weather; freedom from handling overburden or disposing of waste; and minimal requirements for surface space. Today, about 120 stone mines in this country produce more than 5 percent of the total output of crushed stone. This proportion will almost certainly increase during the 1980s.

A valuable by-product of underground mining is the space that is left when mining is completed.

From limestone mine to underground storage, North Kansas City, Missouri. (Photo by J. D. Vineyard.)

When a flat-lying bed of limestone is exposed in a bluff or along a valley wall, it may be possible to extend a mine horizontally, removing the stone from beneath higher ground. A number of such mines in the Kansas City area have been converted into space for cold storage, warehousing, and manufacturing. Access is by truck and railroad car. Typical rooms are 30 feet wide and may be several hundred feet long. The roof, about 12 feet high, is supported by pillars of undisturbed stone. Mining was at first haphazard, but for many years now it has been directed toward later use of the mined-out space.

The underground environment offers several advantages. Space may be purchased or leased at a fraction of the cost of comparable surface facilities. Roof and foundation problems are reduced or eliminated. Floors will support an unlimited weight of machinery or stored goods. Noise and vibration are at a minimum. The facility is fireproof and commands low insurance rates; equipment, records, and materials are secure. Perhaps most important, the cost of heating, air conditioning, and freezing is greatly reduced as compared with installations on the surface.

Mined-out space has been used for such disparate purposes as mushroom growing in New York, preservation of archives in Pennsylvania, and disposal of lime dust in Iowa. Natural gas is stored at many sites, and crude oil in salt cavities and limestone mines in the Gulf Coast region. There is no doubt that we will make increasing use of the underground as suitable space becomes available.

Warehouse in former limestone mine. (Photo by J. D. Vineyard.)

Possibilities offshore. The floor of the sea is a potential source of mineral wealth. From time to time, news stories tell of the discovery of vast areas of metal-bearing lumps or nodules which may be scooped up and brought to the surface. Phosphate-rich nodules have also been found. All these materials, however, lie on the floor of the deep ocean basins beneath several thousand feet of water. Their recovery poses awesome problems of engineering and expense, and their use, if it materializes at all, will be far in the future. Of much more immediate interest are materials that lie on the continental shelf, in less than 300 feet of water and only a few miles from the coast. A potentially major resource in such a setting is sand and gravel.

In Chapter 9 we saw that producers of aggregate often find themselves on the losing side of land-use conflicts in urban areas—either "zoned out of business" or forced to move far away from their markets. An answer to this dilemma, especially along the northeastern seaboard of the United States, may be offshore production.

Preliminary surveys show that there are virtually limitless quantities of sand, and large amounts of more valuable gravel, within reach of the Boston-New York urban corridor. For example, less than 30 miles off the coast of Massachusetts Bay is a deposit containing 1 billion tons of sediment that is at least 60 percent gravel. This deposit occupies an area of 130 square miles and lies at a depth of 160 to 320 feet below sea level. It could readily develop into a major supplier for the greater Boston and Massachusetts shore communities. Another deposit lies just off the coast of New Jersey, within 60 miles of New York City, at a depth of 60 to 130 feet. Its nearshore apex is only 5 miles from land. Leases to dredge this deposit have been requested, but they await the establishment

Underground office. Limestone pillar in background is part of the decor. North Kansas City, Missouri. (Courtesy of Truman Stauffer, Sr.)

of regulatory guidelines by state and federal agencies.

Gravel is less abundant on the continental shelf than sand, and much of it would require longer transport to consuming areas. On the other hand, gravel is more valuable, and distance is a much less significant factor at sea than on land. The capital costs to start commercial dredging would be high, but barging and delivery of gravel to coastal points would be much less expensive than trucking or rail transportation. With efficient technology and good organization, coastal cities should be able to use sea-floor aggregates before the end of the 1980s.

Numerous precedents may be noted. Offshore sand and gravel production around the United Kingdom now amounts to more than 14 million tons per year, or 13 percent of total production, and demand and production are growing. At least 18 percent of Japan's sand and gravel come from the sea. The Netherlands, being without gravel deposits of its own, uses material dredged from shallow waters of the English Channel. Thus, the technology exists. It could readily be adapted to U.S. deposits.

Recycling. Motor fuel, once used, is gone for good: there is no recycled gasoline. Aluminum, copper, and iron, on the other hand, may be reclaimed, and "scrap" metal is a recognized resource. Where do the industrial rocks and minerals fit into the recycling picture?

Certain molding sands may be re-used, and so may clays that promote chemical reactions without themselves entering these reactions. But these are exceptions. Most rocks and minerals that are valued for their physical properties—kaolin in paper, barite in drilling mud, perlite in plaster—lose their identity for good and cannot be reclaimed. And of course, those rocks and minerals that are chemically altered—limestone to lime, sulfur to sulfuric acid, ilmenite to TiO_2—are taken out of circulation with one use. Thus, production of any

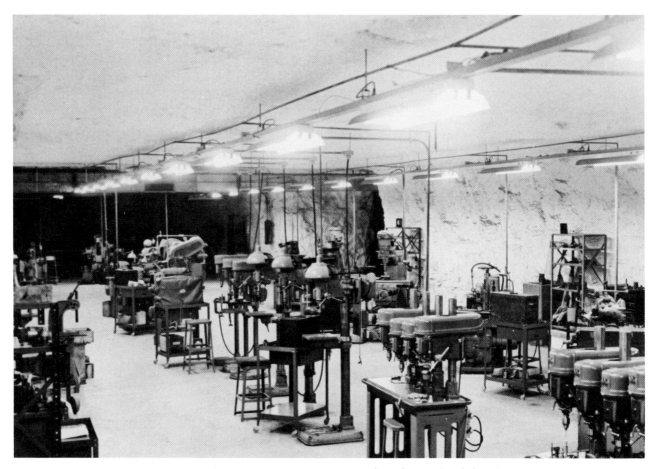

A machine shop 77 feet below the surface. Pillars of the former limestone mine in the background. (Courtesy of Truman Stauffer, Sr.)

nonmetallic raw material practically always means new production from pits, quarries, or mines.

A few mineral-based *products* may go around more than once, however. Perhaps the best-known example is glass; a part of the charge that goes into the melting furnace consists of scrap glass, or cullet. The bottles that people bring to collection centers will be shipped to the nearest glassmaking plant.

A development of the late 1970s was the re-use of broken concrete, suitably crushed and sized, as aggregate in new concrete. "Rubble" from old bituminous-concrete pavement has been found usable in hot-mix paving material. This is made by heating the aggregate and mixing it with hot asphalt before spreading and compacting it. Re-using the asphalt of the old paving is a plus factor, as this petroleum-derived material has become very expensive. An estimate is that by 1985 recy-

cled material will supply 10 percent of the market for hot-mix concrete. Also usable is portland-cement concrete, especially from demolished

Potentially valuable underground space in a still-active limestone mine, eastern Ohio. (Photo by R. S. Wilkinson.)

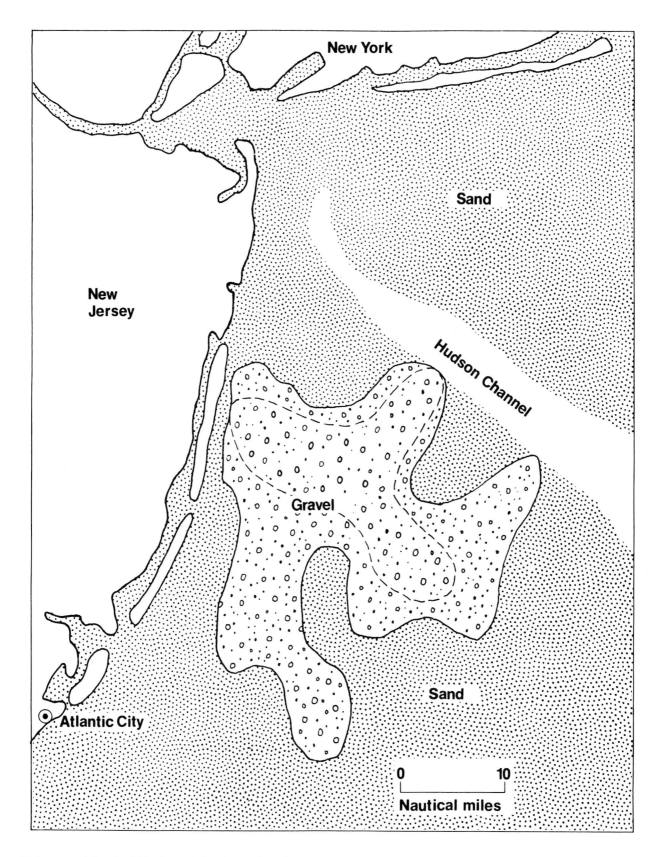

This large gravel deposit off New Jersey, in less than 130 feet of water, is a potential source of aggregate for the New York metropolitan market. Coarsest gravel is inside dashed line. (U.S. Geological Survey.)

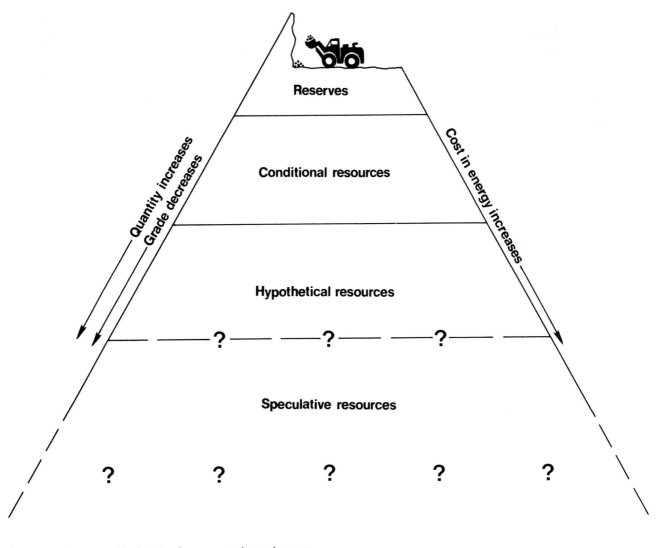

Reserves and resources. The big triangle represents the total amount of a given mineral resource in a region or country. Material that can be profitably mined today constitutes the reserves. Lower-grade conditional resources may be converted into reserves by a rise in price, a technical breakthrough, or lowering of environmental requirements. Hypothetical resources are suspected to exist in known districts; speculative resources are just that.

structures. Since most rubble of this type is generated in cities, the supply is in or near the market area. It may be expected to replace increasing amounts of quarried aggregate as natural deposits are built over or exhausted.

Reserves and Resources

Suppose we asked the president of a manufacturing company, "Looking well into the future, what is your deepest long-term concern about your business?" We might expect him to mention inflation, government regulation, labor troubles, or possibly freight rates or taxes. Now suppose we ask the same question of the president of a mining company. His answer may surprise us. It is likely to consist of the single word *reserves.*

The manufacturer can purchase raw materials in the market as needed, but the miner is *producing* raw material. Since every ton of rock removed from the deposit means one less ton left to be mined, the miner is steadily removing the very reason for his locating there in the first place. He is, as the economist puts it, depleting his capital. Sooner or later, the deposit will be exhausted; that is, there will be no further reserves. This is the problem that is likely to keep the miner awake nights.

Of course, prudent management foresees the problem well ahead of time and takes steps to acquire new reserves. Not only is this likely to be a long and difficult geological task, but it involves economic factors and usually political ones as well. But it must be done: without adequate reserves, a company cannot stay in business.

Reserves are defined as deposits of known size and quality which can be mined profitably at existing price levels with existing technology. Clearly, a reserve is a body of rock, consisting of so many million tons with such and such a purity. But just as surely, it is also an economic entity, defined by existing price levels. If the price of a mineral product falls, it may no longer be possible to mine a given deposit at a profit, and reserves at that place vanish. Conversely, if the price rises—as has happened dramatically with gold, for example—bodies of rock that were formerly of no interest may become minable reserves almost overnight. Still another factor is technology. An improvement in mining or processing methods, or in means of transportation, may convert previously uneconomic deposits into reserves.

Resources constitute the total amount of a given rock or mineral in the earth's crust, or in that part of the crust that is being considered. They include reserves—known, measured, and currently minable—as well as *conditional resources*. These are deposits that are known and have been evaluated but cannot be mined at present for political, economic, or technical reasons. The California phosphate deposit described earlier in this chapter is a good example of the conditional resource. *Hypothetical resources* may reasonably be expected to exist in known districts. *Speculative resources*—most "iffy" of all—may exist in unexplored districts.

The point of giving these definitions is that the two commonly used terms, reserves and resources, do not mean the same thing and should not be used interchangeably. Reserves interest mining companies, but total resources interest governments. Every modern country must have an inventory of its mineral fuels, ore deposits, and industrial rocks and minerals. The more accurate the inventory, the better the planning based on it. Should the government stockpile this mineral in case of emergency? Should it grant producers of that mineral special tax or depletion treatment?

Should it encourage domestic production of another mineral by imposing tariffs on imports? Such questions can be answered with assurance only if the government has good information on the total resources of each rock or mineral, how much is currently recoverable as reserves, how long these reserves will last at present rates of production, and what categories of resources are available for potential future use.

Where do we stand? This country's position as to resources of the industrial rocks and minerals may be summarized as follows.

There are no commercial deposits (that is, no reserves) of five minerals. *Industrial diamond* is imported from Africa—although diamond grit is manufactured in the United States. *Quartz crystal* comes from Brazil. It consists of flawless clear crystalline quartz, which is cut into very thin wafers for use in radios and electronic equipment. Imports are decreasing because of a flourishing synthetic-crystal industry. *Sheet mica* is imported from India, Brazil, and Malagasy. It is punched or cut into shapes for use in electrical and electronic circuits. *Nepheline syenite* is a feldspar-rich igneous rock with the same uses as feldspar. There is one deposit of commercial grade in North America, at Blue Mountain, Ontario, some 75 miles northeast of Toronto. *Graphite* enters the country from Mexico, Sri Lanka, and Malagasy. U.S. deposits of one variety, flake graphite, are sizable but only constitute conditional resources because of high costs.

The United States produces a little *rutile*, but at least 95 percent of our needs come from imports, chiefly Australian. Some 87 percent of the country's *asbestos* is imported from Quebec; 82 percent of the *fluorspar*, mainly from Mexico but also from Spain and Italy; and 66 percent of the *sylvite* and other potassium minerals, from Saskatchewan. Domestic reserves of these four minerals, in the order given, range from slight to large. Considerable *barite* and *gypsum* are imported, not because we lack resources but because certain foreign deposits are pure, close to tidewater, and readily shipped at low cost. The United States is self-sufficient in the other industrial minerals and rocks.

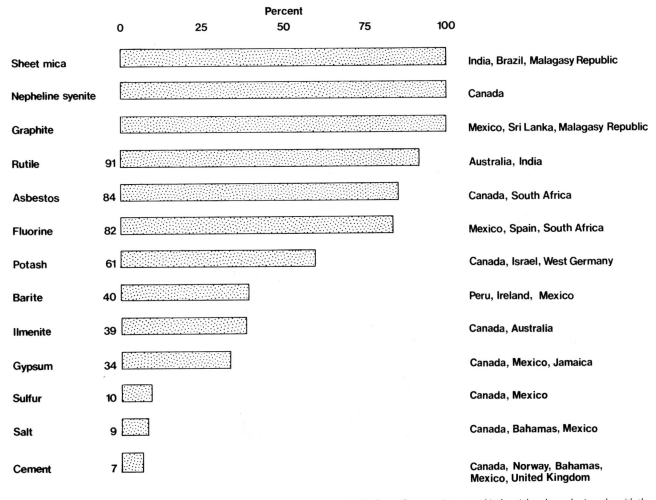

Percent

	0	25	50	75	100	
Sheet mica						India, Brazil, Malagasy Republic
Nepheline syenite						Canada
Graphite						Mexico, Sri Lanka, Malagasy Republic
Rutile	91					Australia, India
Asbestos	84					Canada, South Africa
Fluorine	82					Mexico, Spain, South Africa
Potash	61					Canada, Israel, West Germany
Barite	40					Peru, Ireland, Mexico
Ilmenite	39					Canada, Australia
Gypsum	34					Canada, Mexico, Jamaica
Sulfur	10					Canada, Mexico
Salt	9					Canada, Bahamas, Mexico
Cement	7					Canada, Norway, Bahamas, Mexico, United Kingdom

U.S. dependence on imports of industrial rocks and minerals, with the countries from which the imports come. (U.S. Bureau of Mines.)

How to Look at the Future

This country's resources of certain industrially important rocks are essentially infinite. It is extremely unlikely that we will ever run out of salt, limestone, gypsum, or silica. (Remember the 2,500 cubic miles of high-purity quartz in the St. Peter sandstone alone!) Economic, not geologic, factors will govern our use of these materials. Deposits of some minerals, on the other hand, are sharply limited. For example, a vein system containing fluorspar may extend for a few hundred yards or even a few miles, but the veins will finally pinch out and disappear; the whole district will be shown as hardly more than a short pencil mark on a state or regional map. When such localized deposits are depleted, new ones must be found. This task commonly falls to the geologist. Even though new deposits will probably be harder to find than those we already know about, no shortages are foreseen for most of our industrial minerals. Actually, our mining and quarrying so far have hardly more than scratched the surface of the earth's crust. Furthermore, geologists are learning more about how mineral deposits form and where hidden ones are most likely to be found.

In a third type of deposit, the valuable mineral body fades away gradually into rock of similar but less concentrated composition. Naturally enough, the highest-grade material is removed first. With continued mining, the grade decreases; eventually the ore passes into rock that is not economical to mine. If the deposit is large and the fade-out is gradual, final depletion may be put off for decades. In the Carlsbad potash district of New Mexico, for example, the best sylvite ore has long since been extracted, but several companies are still actively mining lower-grade ore. Exhaustion of the deposits is many years in the future.

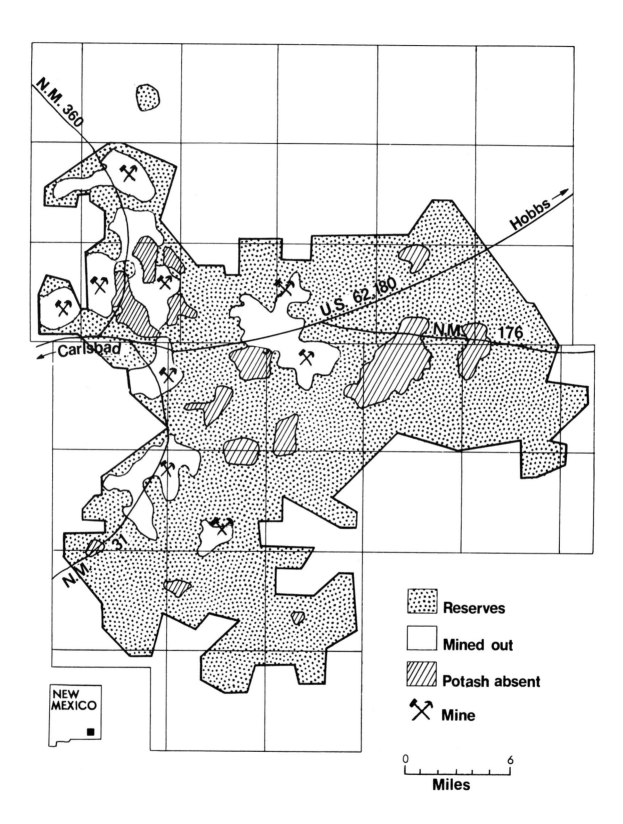

Potash deposits in the subsurface of southeastern New Mexico. Much of the highest-grade material has been mined, but there are still large reserves, and several companies are active in the area. (U.S. Geological Survey.)

Another reason for the Carlsbad district's continued viability is improvements in methods of mining and processing. Indeed in all districts, technology is an important factor in extending mineral reserves. The development of a high-intensity magnetic separator, which allows removal of iron-bearing minerals from Georgia kaolin, has added millions of tons of formerly unusable kaolin to total reserves.

A school of mineral economists has arisen that views technology as the hope of the future. These economists are believers in the horn of plenty; we may call them "cornucopians." They see technological advances making possible the use of lower and lower grades of earth materials, until eventually we will be using common rocks and sea water. (It is possible today—though wildly impractical—to obtain gold from sea water and metallic aluminum and potassium compounds from granite.) Greater pollution is to be expected, say the cornucopians, but this will be controlled technologically. Arctic terrain, wilderness areas, parks and preserves will have to give way, as minerals must be produced wherever found. The enormous demands for energy will be met by nuclear generation. Finally, "some instability in human settlements" will be unavoidable.

This bleak scenario—mineral production at any cost—was fashioned mainly to apply to the metallic ores. The future of the nonmetallics will be somewhat different. High-purity sedimentary rocks, already available in essentially infinite amounts, can be obtained without dire social consequence and are well integrated into the chemical, glass, construction, and other industries. Salt and magnesia are today being extracted from sea water, and this inexhaustible source of supply could be made to yield iodine, bromine, and other elements. Certain nonmetallics could be obtained from common rock—feldspar from granite, for example, or sulfur from anhydrite—but at a high cost in energy. For those nonmetallics whose value depends on special physical properties, however, the cornucopian concept of infinite resources simply does not apply. Vermiculite, barite, or diatomite cannot be produced from ordinary rock, no matter how much country is torn up, no matter how much energy is applied. For certain industrial minerals, we must rely on restricted concentrations—mineral deposits. A combination of geological and technological advances should assure us of an adequate supply well into the future.

Epilogue

The accompanying list gives the 26 rocks and minerals that we have discussed and cites a number of instances at which they enter industry and our daily lives. For every rock and mineral in the list there is a geological story, a sequence of mining, handling, and processing, and more than likely an environmental problem or two. Clearly we have taken a broad view of a complex and intricate subject. Our purpose has simply been to suggest the fascination of a diverse group of earth materials, neither fuel nor metal, that are crucial to our survival and prosperity.

If you have enjoyed this survey of our modern stone age, you may wish to consult some of the books listed under "Further Reading."

The Chief Industrial Rocks and Minerals and Their Major Uses

ASBESTOS: textiles, packings, floor tiles, pipe and panels, brake linings.

BARITE: oil-well drilling mud. *Barium chemicals:* TV tubes, signal flares, fireworks.

BENTONITE: oil-well drilling mud, pelletizing iron ore, foundry molds.

BORAX: glass, flameproofing, soap, boric acid.

DIAMOND: saws, grinding wheels, drill bits, wire-drawing dies.

DIATOMITE: filter aid, filler, paint, insecticide carrier.

DOLOMITE: aggregate, fluxstone. *Dolomitic lime:* refractories.

FELDSPAR: glass, ceramics.

FIRECLAY: refractories.

FLUORSPAR: steelmaking, glass, enamel. *Hydrofluoric acid:* aluminum refining, fluorocarbons.

GRAPHITE: crucibles, refractories, lubricants, pencils, paint.

GYPSUM: wallboard, portland-cement retarder.

ILMENITE: *titanium oxide* for paint pigment.

KAOLIN: paper, china, white tile, paint.

LIMESTONE: aggregate, cement raw material, fluxstone, aglime, ground calcium carbonate, building stone. *Lime:* steelmaking, water treatment, glass, chemicals, "scrubbing" flue gases.

MARBLE: ground calcium carbonate, building stone, monuments and memorials.

PERLITE: lightweight aggregate, insulation, filtration.

PHOSPHATE ROCK: fertilizer. *Phosphorus chemicals:* detergents, cleaners, food additives.

POTASSIUM MINERALS: fertilizer.

SALT: ice control, food processing, metallic-ore refining, water softening, detergents, glazes. *Sodium chemicals:* soda ash, ceramics, detergents, dyes, paper. *Chlorine chemicals:* bleaches, disinfectants, solvents, vinyl chloride.

SAND AND GRAVEL: aggregate.

SANDSTONE: glass, molding sand.

SULFUR: paper, rayon, film, rubber. *Sulfuric acid:* phosphate fertilizer, chemicals, pigments, explosives.

TALC: ceramics, paint, rubber, paper.

TRONA: glass, detergents, water softening, paper, baking soda.

VERMICULITE: insulation, lightweight aggregate, soil conditioner.

Appendix 1.
Further Reading

Bates, R. L. 1969. *Geology of the Industrial Rocks and Minerals*. New York: Dover Publications, Inc. An intermediate-level college textbook that emphasizes origin and occurrence.

Blakey, A. F. 1973. *The Florida Phosphate Industry: A History of the Development and Use of a Vital Mineral*. Cambridge, MA: Harvard University Press. A well-written, illustrated account of the industry from its earliest days.

Boynton, R. S. 1980. *Chemistry and Technology of Lime and Limestone*. 2d ed. New York: John Wiley & Sons. A full discussion, at the technical level, of two essential earth materials. Illustrated.

Brobst, D. A., and Pratt, W. P. 1973. *United States Mineral Resources*. U.S. Geological Survey professional paper 820. Washington, D.C.: Government Printing Office. An overall assessment of this country's mineral resources, including the geologic availability of resources that will be needed in the future.

Cameron, E. N., ed. 1973. *The Mineral Position of the United States, 1975–2000*. Madison: University of Wisconsin Press. Papers by eight authors on such subjects as minerals and how we use them, mineral potential of the United States, impact of environmental concerns, land management, and mining law.

Ellison, S. P., Jr. 1971. *Sulfur in Texas*. Texas Bureau of Economic Geology Handbook no. 2. An illustrated description of Texas sulfur deposits and the recovery of sulfur by the Frasch method.

Flawn, P. T. 1966. *Mineral Resources: Geology, Engineering, Economics, Politics, Law*. Chicago: Rand McNally & Co. A work that relates several special fields "for those seeking a broad background in mineral resources."

Flawn, P. T. 1970. *Environmental Geology: Conservation, Land-Use Planning, and Resource Management*. New York: Harper & Row. A readable discussion of earth materials and processes and how they are modified by the activities of man.

Harben, P. W., ed. 1977. *Raw Materials for the Glass Industry*. London: Metal Bulletin Ltd. A technical but readable survey by several authors.

Harben, P. W., ed. 1978. *Raw Materials for the Oil-well Drilling Industry*. London: Metal Bulletin Ltd. A technical but readable survey by several authors. Includes sections on drilling for oil in the North Sea, the Gulf Coast, and the Middle East.

Kesler, S. E. 1976. *Our Finite Mineral Resources*. New York: McGraw-Hill Book Co. An overview, for the general reader, of the origin, distribution, and remaining supplies of our important mineral resources. The style is informal. Illustrated.

Knill, J. L., ed. 1978. *Industrial Geology*. Oxford: Oxford University Press. Several authors give a picture of geology in the mining and construction industries, especially in Britain. Intended as a text for undergraduates, it relates the study of geology to the real world.

Lefond, S. J., ed. 1975. *Industrial Minerals and Rocks*. 4th ed. New York: American Institute of Mining, Metallurgical and Petroleum Engineers. The authoritative reference work in the field for student or professional.

Manheim, F. T. 1972. *Mineral Resources Off the Northeastern Coast of the United States*. U.S. Geological Survey circular 669. Washington, D.C.: U.S. Geological Survey. Potential resources of sand and gravel for states on the northeastern seaboard. Maps and diagrams.

McDivitt, J. F., and Manners, G. 1974. *Minerals and Men*. Baltimore: Johns Hopkins University Press. "A book for interested, but not expert, readers who want to know more about the non-fuel minerals." (From the Preface.) One chapter is on industrial minerals.

Multhauf, R. P. 1978. *Neptune's Gift: A History of Common Salt*. Baltimore: Johns Hopkins University Press. The story of salt from the earliest days to the present "age of chemical salt." Many illustrations of historical interest.

Park, C. F., Jr. 1968. *Affluence in Jeopardy: Minerals and the Political Economy*. San Francisco: Freeman, Cooper & Co. A discussion of the place of minerals in the industrial economy, their uneven distribution, and potential shortages owing to the world's population growth.

Saskatchewan Department of Mineral Resources. 1973. *Potash in Saskatchewan*. Regina, Saskatchewan: Saskatchewan Department of Mineral Resources. A survey of the origin, geology, history of development, and mining methods of the world's largest potash deposits. Illustrated.

Skinner, B. J. 1969. *Earth Resources*. New York: Prentice-Hall, Inc. An introduction to the geology of metallic ores, industrial minerals, and the mineral fuels. Highly condensed but gives a good bird's-eye view.

Taylor, G. C. 1981 California's diatomite industry. *California Geology* 34:183–192. Occurrence, mining, processing, and use of California diatomite, with a history of the industry.

U.S. Bureau of Mines. 1980. *Mineral Facts and Problems*. U.S. Bureau of Mines bulletin 671. Washington, D.C.: Government Printing Office. The latest edition of a standard reference on mineral resources of the United States.

Utgard, R. O., McKenzie, G. D., and Foley, D. 1978. *Geology in the Urban Environment*. Minneapolis: Burgess Publishing Co. A collection of previously published papers by many authors. Of special interest are Chapter 20, "Mineral Resources for a New Town"; Chapter 21, "Kansas City: A Center for Secondary Use of Mined-Out Space"; and Chapter 22, "Mineral Resources of the San Francisco Bay Region."

Winkler, E. M. 1973. *Stone: Properties, Durability in Man's Environment*. New York: Springer-Verlag. An appraisal, largely technical, of the stability and durability of stone as it has been used in various ways by man. Illustrated.

Yundt, S. E., and Augaitis, B.E.S. 1979. *From Pits to Playgrounds*. Toronto: Ontario Ministry of Natural Resources, Mineral Resources Branch. This little booklet is adequately summarized by its subtitle, "Aggregate Extraction and Pit Rehabilitation in Toronto—An Historical Review." Illustrated with photos and maps.

Appendix 2.
Sources of State Publications

Many of the following state agencies have publications on industrial minerals; the best way to find out is to request a price list of publications.

Geological Survey of Alabama, Drawer O, University, AL 35486

Alaska Division of Geological and Geophysical Surveys, 3001 Porcupine Drive, Anchorage, AK 99501

Arizona Bureau of Geology and Mineral Technology, 845 North Park Avenue, Tucson, AZ 85719

Arkansas Geological Commission, 3815 West Roosevelt Road, Little Rock, AR 72204

California Division of Mines and Geology, 1416 Ninth Street, Room 1341, Sacramento, CA 95814

Colorado Geological Survey, 1313 Sherman Street, Room 715, Denver, CO 80203

Connecticut Geological and Natural History Survey, 165 Capitol Avenue, Room 553, Hartford, CT 06115

Delaware Geological Survey, University of Delaware, Newark, DE 19711

Florida Bureau of Geology, 903 West Tennessee Street, Tallahassee, FL 32304

Georgia Department of Natural Resources, Earth & Water Division, 19 Dr. Martin Luther King Jr. Drive SW, Atlanta, GA 30334

Hawaii Division of Water and Land Development, Box 373, Honolulu, HI 96809

Idaho Bureau of Mines and Geology, Morrill Hall, Moscow, ID 83843

Illinois State Geological Survey, 615 East Peabody Drive, Champaign, IL 61820

Indiana Geological Survey, 611 North Walnut Grove Avenue, Bloomington, IN 47405

Iowa Geological Survey, 123 North Capitol Street, Iowa City, IA 52242

Kansas Geological Survey, 1930 Avenue A, Campus West, Lawrence, KS 66044

Kentucky Geological Survey, University of Kentucky, Lexington, KY 40506

Louisiana Geological Survey, Box G, University Station, Baton Rouge, LA 70803

Maine Geological Survey, State House Station 22, Augusta, ME 04333

Maryland Geological Survey, Johns Hopkins University, Baltimore, MD 21218

Massachusetts Department of Environmental Quality Engineering, Division of Waterways, 1 Winter Street, 7th Floor, Boston, MA 02108

Michigan Geological Survey, Box 30028, Lansing, MI 48909

Minnesota Geological Survey, 1633 Eustis Street, St. Paul, MN 55108

Mississippi Geologic, Economic, and Topographic Survey, Box 4915, Jackson, MS 39216

Missouri Division of Geology and Land Survey, Box 250, Rolla, MO 65401

Montana Bureau of Mines and Geology, Butte, MT 59701

Nebraska Conservation and Survey Division, University of Nebraska, Lincoln, NB 68588

Nevada Bureau of Mines and Geology, University of Nevada, Reno, NV 89557

New Hampshire Department of Resources and Economic Development, University of New Hampshire, Durham, NH 03824

New Jersey Geological Survey, CN-029, Trenton, NJ 08625

New Mexico Bureau of Mines and Mineral Resources, Socorro, NM 87801

New York State Geological Survey, Cultural Education Center, Room 3140, Albany, NY 12230

North Carolina Geological Survey, Box 27687, Raleigh, NC 27611

North Dakota Geological Survey, University Station, Grand Forks, ND 58202

Ohio Division of Geological Survey, Fountain Square, Building B, Columbus, OH 43224

Oklahoma Geological Survey, 830 Van Vleet Oval, Room 163, Norman, OK 73019

Oregon Department of Geology and Mineral Industries, 1005 State Office Building, 1400 Southwest Fifth Avenue, Portland, OR 97201

Pennsylvania Bureau of Topographic and Geologic Survey, Box 2357, Harrisburg, PA 17120

Puerto Rico Servicio Geologico, Apartado 5887, Puerta de Tierra, San Juan, PR 00906

South Carolina Geological Survey, Harbison Forest Road, Columbia, SC 29210

South Dakota Geological Survey, Science Center, University of South Dakota, Vermillion, SD 57069

Tennessee Division of Geology, G-5 State Office Building, Nashville, TN 37219

Texas Bureau of Economic Geology, Box X, University Station, Austin, TX 78712

Utah Geological and Mineral Survey, 606 Black Hawk Way, Salt Lake City, UT 84108

Vermont Geological Survey, Heritage II Office Building, Montpelier, VT 05602

Virginia Division of Mineral Resources, Box 3667, Charlottesville, VA 22903

Washington Division of Geology and Earth Resources, Olympia, WA 98504

West Virginia Geological and Economic Survey, Box 879, Morgantown, WV 26505

Wisconsin Geological and Natural History Survey, 1815 University Avenue, Madison, WI 53706

Wyoming Geological Survey, Box 3008, University Station, Laramie, WY 82071

Appendix 3.
Where To Go and What To See

Historic mine sites and modern mining operations are listed in a series of six illustrated Visitor Guides prepared by the U.S. Bureau of Mines. These may be obtained from the Superintendent of Documents, Government Printing Office, Washington, D.C. 20402, at the prices given below. If you order, be sure to include the GPO stock number, your name and address, and check or money order payable to the Superintendent of Documents.

1. *Mining and Mineral Operations in the New England and Mid-Atlantic States.* GPO stock no. 024-004-01889-5. $2.30.

2. *Mining and Mineral Operations in the South Atlantic States.* GPO stock no. 024-004-01895-0. $2.70.

3. *Mining and Mineral Operations in the North-Central States.* GPO stock no. 024-004-01897-6. $3.25.

4. *Mining and Mineral Operations in the South-Central States.* GPO stock no. 024-004-01903-4. $4.75.

5. *Mining and Mineral Operations in the Rocky Mountain States.* GPO stock no. 024-004-01899-2. $2.40.

6. *Mining and Mineral Operations in the Pacific States.* GPO stock no. 024-004-01872-1. $2.15.

Visitors to Washington may find this publication of interest: U.S. Geological Survey. 1975. *Building Stones of Our Nation's Capital.* Available from the Government Printing Office (see above). GPO stock no. 024-001-02707-1. $1.15.

On the upper level of the Dinosaur Hall in the Smithsonian Museum of Natural History, you can walk through an exhibit called "Fossils as Natural Resources." The exhibit shows samples of limestone, phosphate rock, diatomaceous earth, petroleum, and coal, as well as many products made from each.

A pocket guide to museums in the United States and Canada with earth-science exhibits, providing information on admission fees, tour services, and time schedules, is: Matthews, W. H. III. 1977. *Mineral, Fossil, and Rock Exhibits and Where To See Them.* 2d ed. Available from Publications Department, American Geological Institute, One Skyline Place, 5205 Leesburg Pike, Falls Church, VA 22041. $3.00.

Index